THE
SCUBA DIVING
HANDBOOK

A FIREFLY BOOK

Published by Firefly Books Ltd. 2007

Copyright © 2007 Marshall Editions

First printing

Publisher Cataloging-in-Publication Data (U.S.)

Bantin, John.
    The scuba diving handbook : the complete guide to safe and exciting scuba diving / John Bantin.
[192] p. : ill., col. photos. ; cm.
Includes index.
Summary: Includes equipment and techniques, practical information, the science behind scuba diving, and the best places to dive.
ISBN-13: 978-1-55407-280-4 (pbk.)
ISBN-10: 1-55407-280-8 (pbk.)
1. Scuba diving -- Handbooks, manuals, etc. I. Title.
797.2/3 dc22   GV840.S78.B368 2007

Library and Archives Canada Cataloguing in Publication

Bantin, John
    The scuba diving handbook : the complete guide to safe and exciting scuba diving / John Bantin.
Includes index.
ISBN-13: 978-1-55407-280-4
ISBN-10: 1-55407-280-8
    1. Scuba diving. I. Title.
GV838.672.B365 2007   797.2'3
C2006-906548-9

Published in the United States by
Firefly Books (U.S.) Inc.
P.O. Box 1338, Ellicott Station
Buffalo, New York 14205
Published in Canada by
Firefly Books Ltd.
66 Leek Crescent
Richmond Hill, Ontario L4B 1H1

Conceived, edited and designed in the United Kingdom by
Marshall Editions
The Old Brewery
6 Blundell Street
London N7 9BH
www.quarto.com

Publisher: Richard Green
Commissioning editor: Claudia Martin
Senior designer: Sarah Robson
Project editor: Johanna Geary
Editorial and design: Tall Tree Ltd.
Production: Anna Pauletti

If you want to learn to scuba dive, you must be trained and certified by an instructor following a structured course of PADI, SSI, NAUI, BSAC, or a diving club operating under the auspices of the CMAS, or other internationally recognized training agency. There is no substitute for proper training. The use of scuba equipment without such training and certification can be extremely hazardous, even fatal.

Originated in Hong Kong by Modern Age
Printed in China by Midas Printing
    International Limited

THE
SCUBA DIVING
HANDBOOK

The complete guide to safe and exciting scuba diving

JOHN BANTIN

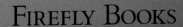

FIREFLY BOOKS

CONTENTS

CONTENTS

WHY GO DIVING?

Scuba divers can't wait to jump off a boat in the middle of the ocean and enter the watery world below.

Watery world

Although we live on the parts of the Earth that protrude above the waves, nearly three-quarters of the planet is underwater. The world beneath the surface of the oceans is as varied as it is on land. The topography includes great mountain ranges, volcanoes and deep valleys. Yet the ocean floor is still largely unexplored and unmapped.

Discovering a mysterious, underwater world should be enough to inspire you to dive, but there are a lot of other reasons to give it a try.

How deep do you go?

People almost always ask those who scuba dive how deep they descend below the surface. Relatively speaking, scuba divers don't go deep. In fact, they hardly penetrate to any depth at all, but they do get an insight into a world that most are unaware of. The majority of marine life congregates in and

It's a wonderful experience to **swim with marine creatures**, such as this giant Napoleon wrasse.

around the first 660 feet (200 m) of depth, close to the shore, and around both natural and humanmade structures. Most of it can be found within the first 100–130 feet (30–40 m) from the surface.

Coral reefs and rocks form natural habitats that give smaller animals protection from larger predators. Modern-day wrecks

may be made of steel, but they perform the same sort of function as far as the marine animals are concerned. They, too, become a habitat for all manner of fish and other marine organisms. It is fascinating to explore these vibrant, underwater homes and learn about the creatures that live there.

Underwater treasure
Another question that people often ask divers is if they have ever found any treasure. Only dreamers think the captain's safe will be full of gold bars, but divers may find objects of interest on wrecks. Older vessels—whether they became shipwrecks because of incompetent seafaring, bad weather or war—were often furnished with a lot of brass fixtures. Some divers have made a hobby of collecting items made of this nonferrous metal from wrecks.

It is a wonderful experience to visit a ghostly ship lying in its watery grave. The coastlines of the world are littered with battered wrecks of ships, many of them relics of the terrible devastation wrought by two world wars.

Incredible creatures
Those who explore the underwater world discover the truth about the creatures that live there. Sharks and other large predators are often portrayed as voracious, undiscerning hunters that eat humans. Few of these much maligned and misrepresented bigger animals are a threat to divers. Most are wary of humans and are easily frightened.

Many divers are willing to spend large amounts of money traveling to places where they can get close to the more spectacular animals, such as sharks and manta rays.

Underwater freedom
Being underwater, weightless in a world where you can travel up or down at a whim, is simply a joyous experience. Many people with mobility disabilities have taken up scuba diving because it frees them from the constraints of gravity. Diving is probably the closest you will ever get to flying without wings!

Sunken shipwrecks are interesting from a historical perspective, but they also quickly become safe havens for all kinds of fish.

THE HISTORY OF DIVING

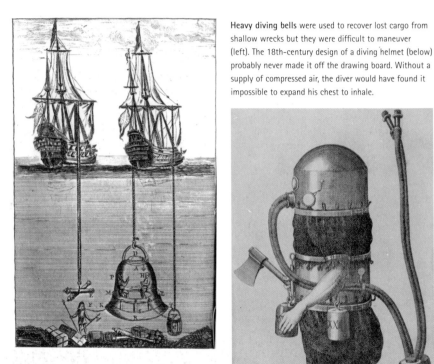

Heavy diving bells were used to recover lost cargo from shallow wrecks but they were difficult to maneuver (left). The 18th-century design of a diving helmet (below) probably never made it off the drawing board. Without a supply of compressed air, the diver would have found it impossible to expand his chest to inhale.

Ancient diving

In ancient times, people used to hunt and gather their food. The Ama people of Japan dived to catch fish by hand and gathered seaweed, sea slugs and shellfish. Legend has it that around 2700 BC, King Gilgamesh of Sumeria searched for a magic plant to give him immortality, which he plucked from the seabed using weights while holding his breath.

The Roman leader Mark Antony is reputed to have employed divers to attach fish to his lines in order to impress his audience with his angling skills.

The activity of divers was limited by their ability to hold their breath. The ancient Greek philosopher Aristotle had the idea of using an upturned cauldron containing air that the diver could place over the head to breathe. But the diver could not have gone more than a few feet deep, and the exhaled carbon dioxide would have soon made the cauldron's use extremely dangerous.

Early inventions

Diving helmets were depicted in 15th-century manuscripts, but they were limited in the same way as Aristotle's cauldron. By the early 16th century, diving bells were invented.

Divers were lowered into the water inside these open-ended chambers and breathed the air that remained at the top of the bell. The bells were intended mainly for the salvage of cargo from shallow wrecks. At this time, divers first noticed how the water level would rise inside the bell as it went deeper. We now know this was due to compression of the air, but it was not until the 17th century that the effect was fully explained by British scientist Robert Boyle. His formula showing the mathematical relationship between pressure and gas volumes (see page 52) is now an important part of the theory of diving, and it also gives us a better understanding of buoyancy.

In 1664, Robert Hooke, an assistant to Boyle, introduced the first Self Contained Underwater Breathing Apparatus (SCUBA) by equipping a diver with air fed to him from sealed lead boxes. There is no record of how successful this project was.

Heavy bells were difficult to maneuver, and soon more lightweight equipment was introduced. In 1720, British inventors John Lethbridge and Jacob Rowe used pressure-proof barrels from which their arms and legs protruded to work as deep as 70 feet (20 m). They could even move themselves small distances around the wrecks they were employed to salvage.

A great advance was made in 1779 with the introduction of a pump used in conjunction with a much smaller diving bell. British engineer John Smeaton was among the first recorded as using one. Pumps were improved, and with a continuous supply of air, bells could stay down safely for longer periods of time.

Many underwater engineering projects, including harbors and breakwaters, were constructed using these methods.

The practice of **Japanese Ama divers** may be as much as 2,000 years old. Most Ama divers are women, and they dive without scuba gear.

THE HISTORY OF DIVING

Siebe-Gorman **standard dress diving suits**, which were commonly used for naval diving, are still used today in some parts of the world.

Diving suits

From the early 19th century, flexible diving suits were introduced that were supplied with air via a hose from a surface pump. These allowed divers to move around more freely.

In 1830, English inventor Charles Deane patented a helmet that was used by his brother, John. It was open at the bottom and allowed pumped air to escape freely. This solved the problem of the buildup of carbon dioxide, the poisonous gas that is the byproduct of metabolism and breathing. The helmet had a short canvas jacket attached. Unfortunately, the helmet was easily displaced, which could result in the diver drowning.

In 1834, an American named Leonard Norcross introduced a closed design with a separate air-escape pipe. It was possibly a British man named Fraser who came up with the idea for an air-escape valve that stopped the suit ballooning as the diver was pulled back up to the surface.

In 1839, Augustus Siebe invented a diving suit that employed a copper helmet, flexible rubberized canvas clothes and heavy boots. It was to be the design that became known as "standard dress" and is still employed today in many parts of the world. It was first brought to prominence when it was used for extensive salvage work on the submerged wreck of the *Royal George*, a British warship that sank tragically in 1782 off Spithead, England, with the loss of 800 lives, including that of Admiral Richard Kempenfelt.

Major inventions

Gas regulators were invented and introduced to help control gas supplies in towns. In 1826, a French inventor named Jean-Jéremie Pouilliot patented a development that could be used as a diver's regulator. It tracked the ambient pressure of depth and only supplied air on demand. The problem was that there was no technology to compress gas and contain it at the pressures that were required to make the equipment viable.

Probably the best-known scuba gear of the 19th century was invented by Benoît Rouquayrol and Auguste Denayrouze in the mid-1800s. In Jules Verne's classic novel, *Twenty Thousand Leagues Under the Sea*, Captain Nemo adopted this equipment.

Most early diving equipment was "open circuit"; that is to say that the air exhaled by the diver bubbled freely away. Because only about one-fifth of air is oxygen and only a small part of the oxygen is used in a breath, open-circuit equipment was very wasteful.

A solution to this problem came with the invention of "closed-circuit" equipment in the middle of the 19th century. In the closed-circuit system, the diver breathed pure oxygen, and the exhaled air was passed over a bed of chemical potash to remove the poisonous carbon dioxide. Introducing a small amount of oxygen from an external supply then made up for the depleted oxygen in the mix, and the diver rebreathed the same gas. English inventor Henry Fleuss patented a successful practical application of the system in 1879.

Closed-circuit equipment emitted few, if any, bubbles that might reveal a diver's presence and was widely adopted by naval divers during World War II. The only problem was its depth limitation. Pure oxygen is now known to become poisonous at depths exceeding 20 feet (6 m), and many divers failed to return from their missions.

World War II military divers using closed-circuit oxygen rebreathers on a two-person underwater chariot.

THE HISTORY OF DIVING

Captain Jacques Cousteau prepares to dive with an early twin-hose regulator.

More advances

In 1905, the British Royal Navy instructed physiologist John Scott Haldane to do some research into the effects on the body of breathing air while under pressure. He experimented with the effects of pressure on live goats to investigate the absorption of nitrogen, which makes up the greater part of the air we breathe. He developed the first-stage decompression tables used by the Royal Navy from 1907 and, later, many other navies.

By the 20th century, steel cylinders were available that could be pumped with gas to high pressures. In 1918, a Japanese inventor, Watanabe Riichi, patented the "peerless respirator" that was used in Pacific pearl harvesting. The diver wore a mask that covered the eyes, nose and mouth. Air flowed from a back-mounted cylinder via a primitive regulator held in the mouth. A self-contained version of the copper-helmeted standard dress soon appeared. Closed-circuit gear using an oxygen/nitrogen mix that was different from air was a secret weapon of World War II.

In France in 1933, Louis de Corlieu introduced what was the forerunner of the modern fin. In 1938, Alexandre Kramarenko marketed a mask and Maxime Forjot patented a simple snorkel tube, probably based on a device used successfully for some time by an English librarian named Butler working at Juan-les-Pins.

In 1943, French diver Georges Commeinhes used his own design of a regulator to descend to 175 feet (53 m) off Marseilles, France. A month later, another French diver, Frédéric Dumas, went to 210 feet (64 m).

Jacques Cousteau

Frédéric Dumas was the chief diver for a team managed by Jacques Cousteau, the French underwater explorer and moviemaker. Dumas used a version of a twin-hose regulator invented by Cousteau and Emile Gagnan called an aqua-lung. Cousteau can be credited with first making the public aware of the underwater world during the 1950s and 1960s. Among other things, Cousteau's films recorded his Conshelf 1 and Conshelf 2 experiments that attempted to investigate life in a long-term undersea habitat. His vessel, an ex-British minesweeper called the *Calypso*, became as famous as he was during its voyages around the world in the pursuit of knowledge. His television series, *The Undersea World of Jacques Cousteau*, was a major international hit.

Another pioneer, Austrian Hans Hass used his own finances to explore the marine world in cooperation with his wife, Lotte.

Scuba diving is a fairly new activity that has only become popular in the last 40 years or so. Developments continue apace, and even today our knowledge is expanding as pioneer divers continue to make new discoveries.

Modern-day divers preparing to go deeper on a leisure dive than Cousteau may have ever imagined possible.

Although it was configured differently, by the 1970s diving equipment functioned much as it does today.

SNORKELING

Snorkeling is an ideal introduction to the world of diving and a wonderful way to explore beneath the waves. It is inexpensive, easy to do and can be enjoyed by swimmers of all ages.

Snorkeling is something worth trying the next time you are near water that is suitable for swimming. It's the sort of activity that most people discover when they are on vacation.

To get your first glimpse of the underwater world, you will need to wear a face mask that allows you to see clearly below the surface. You will also need a snorkel tube that enables you to breathe without having to lift your head up. Both pieces of equipment are usually easy to find and cheap to buy in local stores.

Most of us prefer to swim at the surface of the water. In doing so, most of our energy is consumed in trying to keep our heads unnaturally clear of the water so that we are able to breathe regularly. The snorkel tube frees us from that constraint. As a result, snorkelers discover that they can spend hours simply floating on the surface, relaxed and looking down at what is going on below them.

Snorkeling on the surface and enjoying a wonderful view of the underwater world is a relaxing way to spend a few hours at the beach.

Snorkeling is almost risk-free. You don't even have to be a good swimmer if the sea is calm and there are no currents to worry about. It's something that people of all ages can do, making it an ideal activity for the whole family to enjoy together.

Going below the water

Once you are confident swimming on the surface, it's time to take a breath, hold it and dive down for a closer look at the fascinating things underwater. Swimming beneath the surface requires no additional energy but you will need confidence in your ability to get back to the surface once you feel the need to breathe. A buildup of carbon dioxide triggers your brain to tell you to breathe. Before you can take in more air, you must exhale to get rid of the carbon dioxide, which is a waste gas.

When you break the surface after a short swim underwater, simply tilt your head back and blow the water from your snorkel tube. You can then take another breath before diving below the surface once again.

A warning

Hyperventilation is a deep breathing technique that can be performed before exercising to flush out the normal residual levels of carbon dioxide in the lungs. If the breath-holder starts with lower levels of this waste gas, the urge to breathe is deferred.

However, the body will still use the same quantities of oxygen from the air in the inhaled breath retained in the lungs prior to immersion. If this life-giving oxygen is consumed before the urge to breathe is triggered, hypoxia can occur, resulting in unconsciousness and, if underwater, drowning.

With this in mind, you should never hyperventilate before swimming underwater. Take a normal breath and enjoy a safe and wonderful experience for as long as it lasts.

FREE DIVING

The extreme sport of free diving involves divers getting as deep as possible with only a lungful of air. Participants have to be extremely fit and use special techniques to achieve seemingly impossible depths. Divers Jacques Mayol and Enzo Maiorca first set records of around 330 feet (100 m) and inspired the film *The Big Blue*, but these have been broken many times since by divers Umberto Pelizzari and Pipin Ferreras. Female diver Tanya Streeter broke the men's "no limits" record in 2002 by diving to 525 feet (160 m). The unofficial men's record in this category now exceeds 660 feet (200 m). Don't try this at home!

Umberto Pelizzari dives below the waves on another **free dive**.

TAKING LESSONS

There is a lot to learn about scuba diving and it should be taught in a structured way with a low **student-to-instructor ratio**.

You have probably seen people scuba diving while on your vacation. You may have even enjoyed a "try-dive" session under the strict supervision of a local dive center and experienced breathing underwater for the first time. Now, you may want to go farther.

Unfortunately, scuba diving is not something that can be self-taught, nor can you simply give it a try. The hazards of breathing compressed gas while underwater can be insidious, and there are aspects of it that you would probably never even think of unless you were properly educated in the subject. You need to be taught to scuba dive properly and in a structured way.

Finding a course
There are many routes to learning to scuba dive. You can take a diving course with a dive school while you are on vacation. You can learn closer to home by taking a course and learning the basics in a swimming pool before completing your training in open waters. You can join a club of like-minded people who are only too keen to pass on the knowledge they have and teach you to dive.

Structured courses have been developed by many international training agencies.

DIVING CERTIFICATIONS
Once you achieve your first diving certification, you will realize that it is only the beginning. Entry-level qualifications are simply that. For example, the basic PADI Open Water Diver certification allows you to dive with someone of the same standard in depths up to a maximum of 60 feet (18 m). You'll soon want to go a bit deeper. The PADI Advanced Open Water Diver certification is often misunderstood. It means you will have only advanced slightly. It does, however, certify you to dive to 100 feet (30 m). There are many specialty courses offered, too. These cover every aspect of diving. Schools offering courses by the technical training agencies such as IANTD and TDI also offer training that will teach you to be able to do things you once thought impossible.

The biggest and probably the most famous is the Professional Association of Diving Instructors, more familiarly known as PADI. Other international diving organizations include Scuba Schools International (SSI) and the YMCA, who also provide structured courses, as well as CMAS (Confederation Mondiale des Activities Subaquatiques). They all offer internationally accepted certificates of proficiency at the end of a successfully completed course.

The first thing you need to decide is what environment you would prefer to learn in. Would you prefer to join an amateur club that involves meeting once a week and being taught by volunteer instructors? This can take time, as lessons are spread over many months, but it is cost effective and, in the meantime, you will meet a lot of new friends, many of whom you will go diving with in the future. You can speed things up, at a cost, by going to one of many professional diving schools, often also called dive clubs, and doing an intensive course in the shortest time possible. If you do this in a pool far from the sea, or in other sheltered water, you will need to be referred to another diving school that will help you undertake your qualifying dives in open water.

Another way to learn quickly is to spend a vacation completing a course at a dive center

Learning in the warm and comfortable conditions of a tropical holiday may seem ideal but you will need to **dedicate time** to the course.

based there. This method can raise protests from those with whom you spend your vacation because you will need to dedicate your time to the course. But learning in this way is quick and efficient because you build quickly on what you have learned and tend not to forget anything between lessons. A basic course takes four to five days.

Whether you **learn to dive** at home or while on vacation, it is likely that your initial experiences underwater will occur in the confines of a swimming pool.

KNOW YOUR INSTRUCTOR

Trainee divers learn to trust their instructors implicitly. This trust cuts both ways. Instructors expect would-be divers to be serious in their intention to learn. They should be dedicated to the process, read the recommended books, turn up on time for lessons, listen to what the instructor has to say and watch the demonstrations of skills properly. If they do all this, the training will quickly fall into place.

Certification

Who is the person who is going to teach you to dive? Diving instructors can be certified by many different training agencies to deliver specific courses. Like diving certifications for divers, there are various levels of certification for instructors, too.

A PADI open water diving instructor is certified to teach the basic courses with the help of a dive master. There may be up to six students being taught by one instructor at the same time. A dive master is not an

Even if you are only in shallow water, in the initial moments of training it is important to **identify who is the instructor** and who is there to assist.

During the course, **the instructor is never far away** from those who are learning to dive.

instructor but is there to offer backup and safety cover and often demonstrates various underwater skills so that the instructor is not distracted from keeping an eye on the students in the underwater class.

Sometimes it is difficult for a newcomer to distinguish the job of the instructor from that of the assistant. You should be introduced properly at the beginning of a class so that you have no doubt. Do not be afraid to ask what your instructor's level of certification is.

411553

Classroom lessons will be needed so that you can learn the all-important diving theory.

and the difficulty you have will be down to the quality of the instruction given.

Some instructors like to work to a tight time-scale to meet the basic requirements of your open-water certification. Others will prefer to take more time in order to get you as proficient as possible. Some have a formal approach to training while others are more relaxed. You may prefer to be taught by an instructor of the same sex in a same-sex group. Some diving schools can arrange this.

The vast majority of instructors are passionate about their activity and few do it because it will make them rich. They want you to succeed because a successful student reflects on their own abilities. However, there will always be the occasional rogue instructor or those who are sloppy or incompetent. Instructors should always have proof of their instructor status in the form of an up-to-date qualification card or current certificate. Finally, before you begin lessons, make sure that you are supplied with all the course materials and a dedicated manual that you can keep.

In an amateur club environment, levels of safety are not a legally enforced requirement so you should take care to ensure that you are happy with the volunteer instructor and the method of teaching. You may be learning on a one-to-one basis, which is good, but you may also find yourself in a big group with only one certified instructor. You must decide if that suits you.

Styles of learning

Whether you learn in a club or a professionally run diving school, and regardless of the particular training scheme being followed, the speed at which you learn

Good instructors are passionate about what they teach and will always take the time to explain anything you are unclear about. You may find yourself in a group, but never be afraid to ask questions.

GETTING IN THE WATER

In the pool

When you learn to dive, the first ingredient you need is some water to dive in! Swimming pools are a relatively safe and familiar environment so it makes sense to start there. However, there is a big difference between splashing around on the surface and learning to dive.

You will soon find yourself sitting on the bottom of the pool in unfamiliar surroundings. You'll probably notice things that you hadn't before, such as the fact that the bottom is stepped to provide different depths of water or that the surface viewed from the bottom looks very much like the surface viewed from the top.

It's important to try to think of this small, enclosed body of water as having no edges. Now that you are scuba diving,

A **pool** is a good place to learn basic skills, and you should try to think of it in the same way as you would the ocean.

you don't need to hang on to the edge like you do when you rest during swimming.

You can learn to jump in from the side of a pool just as you jump into the water from a boat. You can also learn to climb out. Most of the basic underwater skills are easy to learn and practice in a swimming pool. And if the pool's heated, you can do it in the best possible comfort.

Lakes and inland bodies of water offer calm controlled conditions that make a good interim step between the pool and the ocean. The temperature of sheltered water might demand that you wear a warm diving suit.

Sheltered water

When you first learn to dive, it's important to do so in water that is sheltered from the effects of weather and tides. Freshwater lakes and protected bays are often used for this purpose.

The main difference between learning to dive in a swimming pool and learning in sheltered water is that you will often need to wear a suit to stop you from getting cold in the natural environment—that is, unless you are learning in a tropical environment where the shallows are warm enough to spend up to an hour or more in without any ill-effects.

You will be invited to walk out through the shallows until you reach water that is deep enough to swim in. Remember, there may be other water users to consider, and you may be distracted by the marine life that passes by. Underwater visibility may not be assured, and if you are learning in a lake that has a muddy bottom, you may have to be cautious about your movements so that not too much sediment is disturbed. You should not stray far away from your instructor.

Open water

Once you've gained some basic skills, it's time to take those first steps into deeper water. Don't worry, it won't be that deep, but it will mean swimming out of your depth.

For your first dives in open water, you will simply repeat all the skills you learned in the pool or in sheltered water. The difference is that you will be asked to do it in a body of water that seems very big in comparison to the confines of a pool.

Your instructor will be there with you every step of the way—or should we say every fin stroke—to ensure that you have no problems. If you do encounter any difficulties, your instructor will quickly intercede to make sure that you don't stop enjoying yourself. Diving instructors are experts at delivering reassurance so you will feel safe and secure at all times. Before long, you'll be a certified diver.

For your first **open-water dive**, the ocean may suddenly seem like a very big place. Don't worry. Your instructor will be with you every step of the way.

BASIC THEORY

Air and water are two very different mediums. Air can be compressed but water cannot. It's important to try to understand the hazards of **breathing compressed air** at any depth.

It's a pity that scuba diving is not simply a matter of swimming around underwater while breathing from an independent air supply. In the early days of the aqua-lung, some adventurous people tried doing this without any basic understanding of the effects of breathing compressed gas while under the very intense pressure caused by water at depth, resulting in some horrible accidents. To dive safely, you will need some understanding of the effects of pressure.

Under pressure

The atmosphere has a weight. Only the gravitational pull of the Earth stops it from floating away into outer space. There is about 60 miles (100 km) of atmosphere above us, and it is pressed down on us with the pressure of 1 atmosphere (1 bar). We are used to it and don't really notice it, but we would surely notice if it wasn't there.

Water is much denser than air. The pressure exerted by only 33 feet (10 m) depth of water equals about the same as 1 atmosphere and, of course, it has the atmosphere pressing down upon it, too. So by going to 33 feet (10 m) deep in water, we effectively double the absolute pressure acting upon us. So why aren't we squashed? Well, that's because liquids cannot be compressed, and we are mainly made up of liquid. But we do have some air spaces within us.

Divers don't go really deep but even at 100 feet (30 m), the pressure is four times greater than it is on the surface. **Breathing equipment** delivers the air at the same pressure as the surroundings.

Air spaces naturally found in the body include the lungs, the spaces connecting the lungs to the nose and mouth, the sinuses and the middle part of the ear.

Gas (air is a mixture of gases) can be compressed. The volume of a gas is inversely proportional to the pressure to which it is subjected. A full, open-ended vessel or a flexible container containing, say, one gallon (4.5 L) of air at the water's surface will contain only half a gallon (2.25 L) of air at 33 feet (10 m) below water, where the pressure is doubled. The mass of air remains the same.

Clever equipment

When we breathe compressed air under water, we breathe it at the same pressure as the water surrounding us. As we continue to breathe and change our depth, the equipment supplying the air automatically alters this pressure to match. However, if we took a breath of compressed air at 33 feet (10 m) deep and held it in our lungs as we ascended to the surface, it would double its volume, doing irreparable, often fatal damage. So the first rule of scuba diving is to breathe normally at all times and to never hold one's breath.

There is also an air space in your ears. You've probably noticed pressure or even pain in your ears when you have swum down a short way under the water. The air gets compressed, and the water distorts your flexible eardrums as it presses on them. The pain results from the imbalance between the water pressure and the air pressure within your ears. You can break these flexible membranes very easily with quite unpleasant side effects. During the first part of your training, you will be taught how to equalize this pressure, and it will become something you do without even thinking about it.

TIP

ALWAYS BREATHE NORMALLY WHILE SCUBA DIVING AND NEVER HOLD YOUR BREATH.

MASKS, FINS AND SNORKELS

Masks, fins and snorkels make up the most basic equipment used by those who want to swim underwater.

Diving masks
Your eyes are designed to work well in air. Try to use them in the much denser medium of water and you'll have difficulty focusing because light bends differently in water. To solve this problem, divers wear a small pocket of air in front of their eyes in the form of a mask.

A mask has a faceplate of tempered glass in one or more sections held by a strong frame. A supple silicone skirt forms a seal between the glass and the diver's face. An adjustable strap holds the mask in place.

Some versions of **split fins** are more efficient than some conventional fins but not all.

Because light bends as it passes from the dense water through the less dense air in the glass, objects look bigger or closer than they really are to divers, and divers also lose their peripheral vision. Good masks have the glass positioned close to the eyes to reduce this problem. The smaller volume of air within the masks also makes them easier to clear if they are flooded with water. Skirts can be transparent or opaque. Opaque ones give a brighter view but are slightly less attractive to wear. If you need prescription lenses, many masks are now available with that option at an additional cost.

Fins and flippers
Fish have fins. Marine mammals have tail fins, too, often in the form of flukes. The forelegs of seals and whales

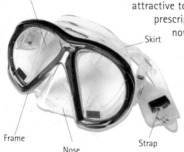

Glass faceplate

Skirt

Frame

Nose pocket

Strap

are modified to form flippers. The swimming aids divers fit to their feet are properly called fins because they enable them to use the muscles in their thighs to propel them through the water.

Adjustable strap

Strap fin

Slipper fin

Whether you prefer to call them "fins," "flukes" or "flippers," this item of equipment enables divers to swim like a fish.

The broad blades of fins allow divers to thrust a larger amount of water than unadorned feet, enabling them to maneuver easily and effectively in the water with minimum effort.

Fins are available in two basic types: slipper and strap. The barefoot diver usually prefers slipper fins, which have an enclosed heel. Those who wear boots usually find the open-heel strap fins more suitable as they can be worn over a boot.

Fins also are available with different-sized blades and varying amounts of flex.

Those divers with strong legs will no doubt relish using fins with large robust blades, but the more relaxed diver will choose a softer or smaller blade.

The latest developments in fin design include split fins. Designers claim these fins are more efficient than traditional ones. Independent tests have proven that some fins with split blades are indeed more efficient, but not all. There are many fins with conventional blades that are just as efficient.

Choosing a snorkel

The snorkel is a tube with a mouthpiece at one end. The tube's ideal length is around 12 inches (30 cm) as this size does not allow carbon doxide to build up. Its ideal diameter is about 1 inch (2.5 cm) as this allows a good flow of air but minimizes the amount of water entering the tube. Some manufacturers make snorkels that are self-draining or have splash guards on top. All snorkels should have a clip to attach to a mask strap.

This snorkel has a **self-draining valve** (1) at the mouthpiece and a **splash guard** at the top of the tube (2).

WETSUITS AND SEMI-DRY SUITS

sea will initially be refreshing for a swimmer, for scuba divers, it will soon make them cold. For this reason, divers normally wear a suit for thermal protection.

Wetsuits

Wetsuits are usually made of neoprene. They are called wetsuits because divers get wet when they swim underwater wearing one. However, the layer of water between the diver and the suit is warmed by the body and, provided it doesn't get flushed out with cold water, it helps keep the diver warm. Of course, the thicker the material of the suit and the more of the body covered, the warmer it keeps the diver. So a 3/16 inch (3 mm) thick "shortie" without arms or legs will not be as warm as a 1/4 inch (5 mm) one-piece, and that will not be as warm as a 3/8 inch (7 mm) suit that has a hood and is worn with a 3/8 inch (7 mm) jacket over top. It's a matter of layering thermal barriers to suit the conditions.

Most divers wear **a suit** of some kind for protection against the loss of body heat and against abrasions (left). **Wetsuits** don't have to look boring (below) but they only work well if they fit properly.

Why wear a suit?

Water conducts heat 25 times more efficiently than air. That's why water is usually used to conduct heat in central heating systems. Your body makes heat to maintain your own body temperature. Water will conduct this heat away from you much quicker than if you were in air of the same temperature. This means that you will get cold after prolonged immersion in any water that is colder than your own body. Divers stay totally submerged for long periods at a time. In hot climates, although a dip in the

People are different, too. A small, compact person with a thick layer of epidermal fat will tend to lose heat more slowly than someone who carries very little fat. Different body types mean divers will choose to use different suits for the same conditions.

Semi-dry suits

Semi-dry suits really are semi-wet. They have smooth skin seals at the wrist, ankle and collar to stop water flushing in and out. They also have a smooth skin flap behind the zipper for the same reason. However, water does get in but in reduced quantities, and often divers can feel warmer in a good,

A **semi-dry suit** can keep you warmer than a wetsuit because less water can get in past its seals.

well-fitting semi-dry suit than in a wetsuit. Some suits have thicker neoprene in areas that do not need to be flexible, combined with lighter weight neoprene at joints like elbows and knees.

When choosing a suit, get one that fits you. To work well, a wetsuit should be a good fit, although modern super-stretch neoprene makes this less of a problem than it used to be. Female divers will want a suit that is specifically designed for their shape. The designers of wetsuits have recently woken up to the fact that most women have a different shape than men!

A full suit protects the wearer from abrasions caused by accidental contact with rocks, coral or the rusting metal of shipwrecks, and it prevents stings from plankton and jellyfish.

WHAT TO WEAR WHEN AND WHERE

If you dive in temperate waters, such as those found in northern California in summer, the Mediterranean in winter, or southern Australia and New Zealand all year round, you will need to have the full protection of a 3/8 inch (7 mm) full-length semi-dry suit with 3/8 inch (7 mm) jacket worn over it. The Red Sea and the seas around South Africa in winter require a 3/8 inch (7 mm) full-length semi-dry suit. A 1/4 inch (5 mm) full-length semi-dry suit is suitable for diving in the Mediterranean in summer, the eastern Pacific, northern Australia and places that are swept by strong ocean currents. A 3/16 inch (3 mm) full-length wetsuit is fine for the Caribbean, the Red Sea in summer and waters in most tropical zones that are not subject to strong currents.

This **semi-dry suit** is made from 3/8-inch (1 cm) thick neoprene. It has an equally thick jacket worn over it with an attached hood, and extra-thick panels clearly visible around the lungs and kidneys for even better insulation.

DRYSUITS

Functions of a drysuit

Drysuits are used in temperate climates where the water may not be very warm.

The core function of a drysuit is to keep you dry. To do this, it must fit you well, have efficient seals at the neck and wrists, and be made of a material that does not allow water to pass through it. The material must also be hard wearing because if it gets punctured even with the minutest hole, at the pressure encountered at depth, water will gush in.

A drysuit gets compressed as you go deeper, so a method of inflating the suit with air to keep its volume constant is needed. Drysuits have a direct-feed inflation valve, which is fed with air from a hose connected to a supply of gas, normally the main air supply of the diver. In this way, buoyancy can usually be controlled without resorting to use of the buoyancy compensator (BC).

The reduction of pressure during an ascent causes the air in the suit to expand. This air needs to be vented, and a drysuit has a dump valve for this purpose. Cuff dumps are operated manually, while auto dumps,

The correct use of a membrane-type drysuit means that buoyancy can be perfectly controlled without resorting to use of the BC while underwater.

more properly called constant-volume dumps, vent air automatically. The position of a dump valve is critical and should be at the highest point that air can rise to in the suit, which is normally the upper shoulder.

What are they made of?

Drysuits are made of a variety of materials, including thick neoprene, crushed neoprene, compressed neoprene and laminated layers of butyl rubber or another rubberized material. Trilaminate suits and other membrane-type suits do not get compressed at depth so are easier to maintain constant buoyancy. Thick neoprene suits often need to be used in conjunction with air in the BC. Seals can be made either of latex rubber or thicker neoprene. The former tends to be more watertight but is also more fragile. The latter tends to be more comfortable but a little damp.

A diagonal **front-entry drysuit** fits snugly thanks to its telescopic body and internal braces.

DRYSUIT VALVES
Drysuit inflation valves (below) are normally mounted on the chest area of the suit and are connected via a hose to the diver's main supply. To add air, the diver presses the inflation button. Air is usually added in short bursts.

A cuff dump is operated by raising the arm to the highest point of the suit. An auto dump (below) is often mounted on the upper shoulder.

Other features
To make a drysuit less bulky, manufacturers have come up with several design features, such as telescopic bodies worn with a tuck and elasticated or ruched waists. Internal suspenders can make them more comfortable.

A diver gets into a drysuit through an opening that is closed with a watertight zipper. This can be positioned either across the shoulders or diagonally across the chest. So-called front-entry, self-donning suits are rarely that easy to put on, and divers always seem to need the help of a buddy to close the zipper that last couple of inches.

Drysuits usually have integrated boots or closed sockends for use with separate hiking-style boots. A wet hood can be worn. Fit is very important, and if you are not a regular size, you will need a made-to-measure suit.

They may keep the diver dry, but drysuits do little to keep a diver warm in the water. Thermal insulation is provided by an undersuit that pulls away sweat on the inner surface and uses modern fibers to insulate the diver from the cold.

HOODS AND GLOVES

A hood is a low-tech solution to keeping heat in, and underwater it soon becomes a part of you.

Head cover

Our brains need a plentiful supply of blood to work properly but can't do so in the cold. Yet few of us have much naturally provided thermal insulation in that area.

We lose a lot of body heat through our heads, so it makes sense to provide this area with its own extra insulation before covering any other part of your body. Convention dictates, however, that we look rather silly if we wear a hood and no suit—so divers tend to dress in a diving suit as a first step to keeping warm.

A hood is a low-tech solution to keeping warm so do not forget to take one along with you. If you find you feel cold in your suit alone, adding a hood can make a big difference to your comfort.

Some hoods have a seal around the neck and face to stop cold water from flushing through, but it is essential to allow water to reach your ears so that you can equalize the pressure as you go deeper. The face seal has a double function in that it stops exhaled air from entering and lodging in the top of the hood (giving the diver a pointy-headed effect). Some divers simply cut a small hole to allow any such air to escape, while others have hoods fitted with a small valve or a hole hidden behind a secondary internal flap.

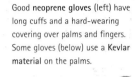

Wearing gloves

When you get cold, your body automatically reduces the blood supply to your extremities, such as your hands and feet. For this reason, in the freezing conditions found at the tops of high mountains or in the Antarctic, mountaineers and explorers can lose fingers or toes to frostbite. Even in the less extreme winters in temperate climates, gloves are often a necessary item of clothing when venturing outdoors.

If you are diving in cold conditions, wearing a warm pair of gloves is sensible. You may even choose to wear a pair of thick, wool gloves under a pair of diver's dry gloves that keep the water out completely. If you are moving around a wreckage that has rusty or jagged steel edges, a strong pair of diving gloves is probably essential. If you are diving in an area where the currents are really fierce, a tough pair of gloves is useful to allow you to cling on to the rocky substrate and stay in one place.

Gloves are available in a variety of materials, such as light canvas, soft neoprene, almost indestructible Kevlar and even stainless steel chain mail.

Good **neoprene gloves** (left) have long cuffs and a hard-wearing covering over palms and fingers. Some gloves (below) use a **Kevlar material** on the palms.

Latex dry gloves are integrated with a drysuit cuff via a ring system, so that both suit and gloves share the same internal airspace.

When not to wear gloves

Although wearing gloves makes sense in many diving situations, in some places in the world the use of gloves while scuba diving is banned. This is because the underwater ecosystem is fragile. Years ago, divers wore gloves to protect them from touching stinging corals. Today, divers are banned from wearing gloves in order to protect the corals from damage. The rule is: if you do not know what it is, do not touch it. It may sting you or it may not, but at least you won't hurt it. Dive with your eyes, not your hands.

These gloves have a natural **Merino wool lining** that makes them suitable for use in cold conditions.

31

REGULATORS AND PRESSURE GAUGES

A **typical regulator** reduces the pressure of the air in the tank in two stages so that, at the mouthpiece, it exactly matches the pressure of the water surrounding it.

Mouthpiece

First-stage

Second-stage

Understanding regulators

A regulator is a device that allows you to breathe air from a tank. The modern two-stage scuba-diving regulator valve is a relatively simple item of engineering. Its function is to reduce the pressure of the gas being delivered from the tank through the first-stage to around 120 pounds per square inch (psi, 8 bars) to 150 psi (10 bars) more than ambient pressure. It then reduces the pressure further, at the second-stage, to match the surrounding water pressure. In this way, there is virtually no effort to inhale. The regulator then has to allow the user to exhale the unused part of the inhaled gas. Exhaled air is simply bubbled out into the water. The idea is to make breathing as natural as possible.

Regulators vary in price considerably. You could be forgiven for thinking that the best performing regulator is the most expensive and that the cheapest is hard to breathe through, but this is not true. Unfortunately, there is no way of finding out which one is best before you buy—you can't try a regulator in the store. What you can examine is the specification of a regulator, its design features, what it's made of and how well it has been finished.

This **regulator first-stage** (1) has a DIN-fitting tank connection but is shown with an adaptor (2) that allows it to fit international A-clamp type tanks.

Regulators employ either a diaphragm or a piston mechanism in the first-stage. In general, pistons give high performance but are less suitable than diaphragm designs for use in cold, freshwater since their working parts come into contact with water.

A balanced first-stage will keep demand pressure constant regardless of what the pressure of the air is in the tank, which means it will not be more difficult to breathe as the tank empties. Very cheap regulators tend to have unbalanced first-stages.

INTERNATIONAL A-CLAMP AND DIN CONNECTIONS

The international A-clamp connection (1) between the regulator first-stage and the tank valve is universally accepted around the world. The A-clamp presses and holds the two parts together with an air-tight seal provided by a small rubber O-ring.

Regulators with a screw-in DIN connection (2) have their own "trapped" O-ring which offers some advantages in precision fitting. However, DIN connections can be less resilient to rough handling. A 4,300-psi (300-bar) DIN connection is the only type of fitting possible if you want to use gas supplies of higher pressure than 3,300 psi (230 bars), and in technical diving (a form of diving that uses special techniques to extend diving depths). The bottom picture shows a tank that is fitted with regulators with each connection.

The second-stage is held in the mouth. Most mouthpieces are made from plastic because it is light. However, plastic does not have any heat-sink qualities (which would enable it to absorb heat). This is important if the diver intends to use the regulator in cold, fresh water. Some manufacturers add metal inserts to allow for this while others make the whole item from metal.

Some regulators have a breathing-resistance adjustment knob that can be used to vary the amount of effort needed to crack open the valve with the initial part of an inhalation.

The clean flow of air within the body of the second-stage can cause a venturi effect (which is what happens when wind increases velocity because of a constricted flow). This effect can make breathing easier, but it can also cause exponential free-flows under certain conditions. Some regulators have a venturi plus/minus switch that positions a vane within the flow to disrupt it.

The design and function of the purge valve can be crucial, too. It's used to give a boost of air to clear water from the mouthpiece should it flood. The design of the exhaust "T" is important because you don't want to have to look through a curtain of your own exhaled bubbles.

Regulators have ports that allow hoses for ancillary equipment to be fitted. One of these is the pressure gauge. It shows the pressure of air remaining in the tank and is used like a fuel gauge. Your instructor will teach you how to manage your air supplies.

Indicator

Final quarter mark

The **pressure gauge** may be regarded as a contents gauge. The red section indicates the final quarter.

BUOYANCY CONTROL DEVICES

Keeping buoyant

In its simplest form, a buoyancy compensator, or BC, is merely a bag that you can put air into during the descent and let air out of as you come back up. Why do you need to do that? Although your body is more or less neutrally buoyant, it is not compressible like most of your equipment. However, the air in the tiny bubbles that form the neoprene of your suit is.

As you go deeper, your suit compresses with the increasing pressure of depth and you lose buoyancy because it displaces less water. You appear to get heavier. As you come up again, it regains its volume and recovers its buoyancy. By adding air to a BC or letting it out according to your circumstances, you can compensate for any changes in pressure.

This is a typical **jacket-style BC** that also gives surface buoyancy at the lower front.

Diving can be effortless if a **buoyancy compensator** is worn and used correctly

To make it convenient to use, the buoyancy cell is contrived to be part of the equipment you wear. The air you put into it underwater rises to the highest point, which is normally at your back, near the top of your shoulders. This air comes from a hose fitted between the BC and your regulator. Small amounts are fed into the BC as and when needed from your main supply.

The BC has another important function. It can be filled to its maximum capacity so that it acts as a flotation device for the diver. This means that you can remain comfortably at the surface when required.

An upper dump-valve can be operated by pulling on the corrugated hose.

The direct-feed control is fed with air from the diver's tank.

Oral inflation valve

34

If you are at the surface but your tank is out of air, you blow into the BC via a flexible corrugated hose and an oral inflation valve.

To let air out, most BCs are equipped with dump-valves operated either by pulling on the corrugated hose or by pulling on a separate cord and toggle or both. As a last resort, you can always lift the corrugated hose and let the air out by opening the oral inflation valve. However, this will let water

A **single-bag BC** gives the diver a sleek line in the water.

WHY CHOOSE A WING?

A wing-style BC is used in exactly the same way as any other BC but with the buoyancy cell entirely at the back. This allows a huge amount of lift, while keeping the front part of the harness clear for attaching equipment. This type of BC has proved popular with technical divers who clip on lots of extra equipment. The masses of lift provided by a big air-cell can count when diving with multiple tanks, but not so much at the surface where a lot of the wing is out of the water.

back in the other way, which only adds to the weight of your equipment when you climb out of the water.

Types of BC

BCs come in various shapes. Some are jackets, whereas others are simply large bags attached to the back of the harness. The jacket BCs can keep more air low down under the water when the diver is bobbing at the surface. The bag BCs, or "wings," can be large and so give far greater maximum flotation.

Some BCs are made with a single bag construction, whereas others are composed of a bag within an outer lining. The first type gives a sleeker more aqua-dynamic line, whereas the second is more hard wearing.

Useful functions

Probably the most important function of a BC is that it holds the tank on your back. Then there are all the peripheral functions that a BC might have, such as integrated weight pockets, trim weight pockets and pockets for carrying things in. Stainless steel D-rings allow you to clip on items, such as lights, and to clip away gauges on hoses.

WATCHES, DEPTH GAUGES AND COMPASSES

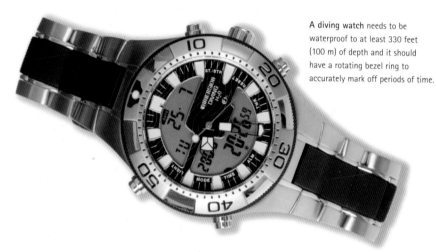

A **diving watch** needs to be waterproof to at least 330 feet (100 m) of depth and it should have a rotating bezel ring to accurately mark off periods of time.

Essential further information for divers

As well as knowing the amount of air in their tank, the three basic pieces of information that divers need to know are: the amount of time they have spent underwater, the depth of the dive and their direction. For this, divers need to time the dive. Divers also need to be able to measure depth and know the maximum depth achieved. Finally, divers need to be able to navigate underwater.

It may be obvious why divers need to navigate, but why do they need to know depth and time? The tissues of the body absorb the nitrogen in the air we breathe underwater. The deeper we go, the greater this effect. We need to be able to calculate the maximum time we can stay at any given depth without ill effect. There are diving tables that give these figures (see page 35).

Diving watches

A suitable watch is needed to time the dive. It should be waterproof to a maximum depth of at least 330 feet (100 m).

This is not because a diver will go to that depth, but because of a curious system used by watchmakers to calibrate their watches.

Divers need watches that are more than just water resistant. A watch that claims to be water resistant to 100 feet (30 m) is great for wearing while washing the car, but it is not good for any other water-related activity. The watchmaker's code for water resistance relates to static-water testing only and doesn't mean that a watch is suitable as a diver's watch.

A diving watch needs to have an omni-directional bezel that can be used to mark the moment that a diver left the surface. The bezel should move in only one direction so that if it gets accidentally hit it can't move to a later start time. The watch face should allow you to read the time even when the water clarity is not good.

Depth gauges

A depth gauge is as important to a diver as an altimeter is to an air pilot. This instrument is also a navigation tool because it can tell divers if they are traveling up or down through the water column.

A good depth gauge will include a method of recording the maximum depth achieved during the dive.

A **depth gauge** (center) is often included in an instrument console together with the pressure gauge and a diving compass.

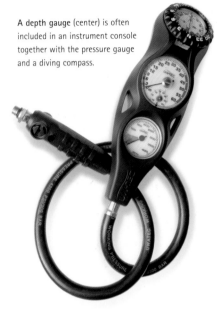

Compasses

A conventional compass is used underwater in exactly the same way as it is used on land except that a diver has to be sure to hold it in the right way.

A compass has a magnetic pointer that must be allowed to swing. Some compasses have a sight glass to allow you to read off a bearing while holding it up in front of you.

The **diving compass** can either be of the simple magnetic type (left) or a more sophisticated electronic instrument (right).

NO-STOP DIVE TIMES

Working for the British Navy, Dr. John Scott Haldane created the first tables for how long an average person can stay underwater at different depths and come directly back to the surface without stopping. Naturally, the rate of ascent is crucial, too. He determined a guide to safe no-stop diving times at different depths, followed by an ascent-rate of 60 feet (18 m) per minute. It's known as the RNPL table and allows a no-stop dive for 23 minutes to 88 feet (27 m).

There are now many different tables. The US Navy produced its own set of figures that claim you can dive to 88 feet (27 m) for 30 minutes without stopping. Later, the Swiss physicist Bühlmann came up with a new table with an ascent rate of 33 feet (10 m) per minute and a no-stop time of 21 minutes at 88 feet (27 m). PADI commissioned its own Recreational Dive Planner, which allows 25 minutes at 88 feet (27 m).

Often the depth gauge and compass are included in a single console at the end of a hose together with the tank pressure gauge. The electronic revolution has not only given us watches, both analog and digital, but we can now equip ourselves with electronic compasses that work underwater, too. One very popular type is combined in a watch-sized diving computer.

TIP

DEPTH, ELAPSED TIME AND DIRECTION FORM ESSENTIAL INFORMATION TO THE DIVER.

DIVING COMPUTERS

This photograph was taken during a diving magazine's side-by-side **comparison test** of different models.

Underwater computers

Miniature electronics have revolutionized everyday life and have made their presence felt in the world of diving, too. It's hard to believe there was a time when divers did not carry computers with them to manage their dives. Divers need to know how long they dive for and to what depths. They need to know how much no-stop diving time they have left (the maximum considered safe for a certain depth), what stops may be needed during an ascent and for how long. They also need to know how fast they are ascending, what is their current depth and what was their maximum depth. Finally, they need to take into consideration the previous dive before planning the next.

Today, the magic of the microchip takes care of all that. A diver simply wears a small

DECOMPRESSION ALGORITHMS

An algorithm is the calculation that sets depth against time and combines this with a set of theoretical tissue-models that go some way to representing the different tissue types in your body.

These model tissues have "half-times," which are the time it takes for them to have absorbed half the volume of gas that they still need to absorb to become saturated. These vary from short ones that represent the fast tissues like the blood to long ones representing the slow-to-desaturate tissues such as those found in bones. The calculation is also modified by other varying factors. Some computers use many different tissue models in their algorithms, whereas others use far fewer.

unit on the wrist and follows the instructions continuously displayed. A computer is ideal for multilevel diving. It keeps precise track of reducing no-stop times and decompression-stop requirements, whatever the dive profile.

No serious diver should be equipped without a diving computer, and there are many to choose from. Diving computers probably represent the single most important advance in diving equipment since the invention of the aqua-lung.

Special functions of dive computers
Since many technical divers use nitrox (an air mix with increased oxygen and decreased nitrogen), most diving computers can accommodate the extra parameters that nitrox introduces. They take care of maximum operating depths for a given maximum ppO_2 (partial pressure of oxygen), and track oxygen toxicity, as well as being able to account for the advantage—the increased tolerance to breathing gas at depth.

Some computers can track decompression when a diver uses more than one nitrox mix during a dive, or even uses a part-helium mix instead. There are even computers that can take into account the amount of gas you are breathing and estimate how long the remainder in your tank will last at that depth. Some are connected to your tank by a high-pressure hose, whereas others use a radio transmitter to send messages to a wrist unit.

Miniaturized devices
Many dive computers are only the size of a large watch yet their displays are easy to read. They can be very stylish and conveniently double as an everyday watch.

The microchip brings vast numbers of peripheral functions, too. All manner of alarms and personal preferences can be selected, including the way your decompression is calculated.

Some computers offer a choice of algorithms and others even give the diver the choice of making a deep-stop on the way up from a square-profile dive instead of heading directly for the shallows.

There are a few computers that can be adjusted to work with constant partial pressure of a gas rather than the percentage of oxygen against depth. These are for use by closed-circuit rebreather divers.

Finally, most diving computers allow you to interface with a PC so that you can download your dive information and go over what you did in detail later.

At depth, this **computer** displays the actual depth and elapsed dive time, the maximum depth achieved and the time it will take to safely ascend to the surface.

Back at the surface, the diving computer remembers and **displays details** of the dive that can be written down by hand or downloaded to a computer.

> **TIP**
>
> UNDERSTAND THE SIGNIFICANCE OF THE INFORMATION YOUR COMPUTER TELLS YOU.

A small folding knife that has a blade with a choice of edges can be a lifesaver to a diver tangled in fishing line.

Carrying a knife

Divers use knives as tools for getting out of trouble. In the days when divers wore brass helmets and lead boots, a large brass-handled knife strapped to the chest was essential. The knife was there in case the lifeline got snagged and the diver had to cut the line.

Today, diving in low-visibility water on wrecks that are popular fishing sites is dangerous for a diver, as he or she may become snagged in the lines. This is particularly a risk with monofilament lines that are almost invisible underwater. In this case, a knife can save a life.

Small, sharp knives, equipped with line cutters are the most useful. In fact, a simple line cutter can be better than a knife. Many divers now choose to include several smaller knives in various areas of their diving gear so

that, if they need a knife, they can always reach for one.

Divers' knives are not weapons and should never be used as such. In some countries, there are laws regarding the carrying of knives. Be sure to keep your knife with your diving kit and never carry it separately to avoid potential misunderstanding of its purpose.

An extremely **loud whistle** (1) operates by using air from the BC direct-feed supply (2).

A **yellow flag** on an extending pole can often be seen for several miles.

Some sensible divers carry a flag on an extending pole. It easily rolls up and fits under an elastic strap alongside the tank. When the time comes to deploy it, the large flag can be clearly seen from even several miles over the wave tops.

Various colors are available and everyone has their own ideas, but students at Heriott-Watt University in Edinburgh, Scotland, made a study of the subject and found that bright yellow proved to be the most visible color for use at sea.

Some divers use an inflatable safety "sausage," which is described on page 50.

Knives often have other functions provided by screwdriver ends, shackle keys and so on. For dealing with an entanglement in a fishing line, you may even be better off using scissors.

Strobes

Another item of safety equipment is a flashing underwater strobe. It runs for many hours on a small battery, yet emits a water-piercing white flash. It can mark your position to another diver in low visibility conditions or even to those on the surface during nighttime diving. When you surface at night, a flashing strobe will allow the crew of the pickup boat to find you easily. Of course, if you have been using a light underwater you can always use that instead.

Other ways of attracting attention

One of the biggest hazards for divers is getting lost on the surface after a dive is finished. The ocean is a very big place and waves can easily obscure the head of a diver, so you need to be able to mark where you are in the water clearly. One way to attract attention is to use a very loud whistle powered by high–pressure air from your tank.

A **security strobe** (left) makes a good beacon at night. The **steady beacon** (right) is good for buddy marking.

DIVING LIGHTS

A powerful light will illuminate parts of a tropical reef in vibrant color.

Why use a light?

If you are diving in conditions with poor visibility it will be dark underwater. A diving light will help you see and be seen. If you are going to explore inside a shipwreck, a light (plus a spare) is essential. If you are diving at night, a light as well as a stand-by securely clipped off in a pocket must be part of your equipment. However, you don't need to carry a really bright light for either of those purposes.

You may be surprised to learn that a powerful light will also help you enjoy a daylight dive on a tropical reef in brilliant sunlight. This is because water filters out the color from the ambient light at depth and everything looks muted, that is, until you shine a powerful beam of white light on it. Objects that look brown or black often turn out to be a vibrant crimson once illuminated by a light source.

Types of diving lights

Cheaper diving lights use readily available alkaline dry-cell batteries, and as each cell equals 1.5 volts, it is easy to work out the maximum voltage available. These

LOTS OF CHOICE

All you used to need to know about underwater lights was their wattage. Now there are different types of bulbs: halogen, HID (high intensity discharge), and LED (light emitting diode). HID lights give an amazing output of cold light. LED-equipped lights give a similar color beam but are less bright. They have a burn time of many hours per set of batteries or charge. Light output is now measured in lumens, not power consumption. The battery voltage can give a good idea of how bright a light is, but the design of the reflector determines how much of that light gets projected forward.

inexpensive models have a variety of methods of switching on and off, some of which are liable to allow water into the light and flood it.

Rechargeable cells include Ni-cad and NiMh. They are available in both 6-volt and 12-volt sizes. NiMH cells have advantages over old-fashioned Ni-cads in that they can be recharged at any state without creating a memory effect. That means you can always be sure to start a dive with a fully charged light.

The more expensive lights usually have aluminum bodies and large batteries. This means they often still weigh quite a lot even when submerged. The better ones come with neoprene sleeves to help negate this effect.

Keeping water out of airspaces in equipment that you submerge to great pressure, as you do when you go diving, is a problem. The more openings a light has in its case, the more opportunities there are for a disastrous leak. Openings are sealed using neoprene O-rings. Lights that have user serviceable O-rings can be problematic if the O-ring is not kept scrupulously clean and lightly greased.

Some lights have to be opened up to recharge them, whereas others can be

The **aluminum light** (left) has a neoprene cover that goes some way to making it more buoyant, whereas the plastic construction of the other (below) is neutrally buoyant, meaning it will neither sink nor float.

charged using external connections that neatly avoid the problems involved in opening up the light.

Umbilical lights separate the heavy battery pack from the bulb head. This means the battery pack replaces the lead on your belt and the bulb head is light and easy to handle. Big handheld lights tend to be heavy, which can lead to buoyancy problems if you put one down during a dive.

A **coral reef** is an exceedingly colorful place, but you might not ever notice unless you shine a powerful white light at it from close by.

WEIGHTS AND WEIGHTBELTS

Weighed down

Most people are naturally neutrally buoyant. With a normal relaxed lung volume, they neither float nor sink. If they take a deep breath, they will float. If they empty their lungs, they will sink.

As soon as a diver puts on a diving suit, more water is displaced by the suit and the diver will float. It is necessary to strap on some ballast (weight) to counteract the buoyancy of the suit. The most convenient and common type of weight is lead.

Most divers simply thread their block-style lead weights onto a length of 2-inch (5-cm) webbing and use it as a belt. If you require more comfort than a belt provides, a harness can help.

Another way to carry lead is in the form of lead shot, which requires a shot belt or a belt that takes shot in pouches. If you use a lightweight aluminum cylinder, you may prefer to strap some V-shaped lead to that.

Some divers like to **attach lead to their ankles** to compensate for buoyant legs, and to their tanks if they are lightweight.

Using the **minimum amount of lead** allows the diver to be neutrally buoyant without too much air in the BC.

There are other systems that allow you to strap part of the weight to your tank. Otherwise it should be possible to release all ballast in an emergency—that's why all systems have a quick-release buckle.

Many variables

Divers will need to work out how much lead to carry, but there are many factors to take into account when making this decision. One of these is the size and thickness of your suit.

This **metal weightbelt buckle** has a security pin that must be pulled before it can be released in an emergency.

This **novel weightbelt buckle** has a rip-away release separate from its adjustment.

A thick neoprene diving suit with a bulky jacket over it displaces more water than a thin suit alone, making you more buoyant. You will, therefore, need more lead if you are wearing a thicker suit.

The buoyancy of any equipment is also important. Aluminum tanks can be almost neutral, whereas steel tanks are always very heavy even when immersed. Also the air in the tank has weight. A full 80-cubic-foot (12-L) cylinder is over 6 pounds (3 kg) heavier than it is when it is empty.

The density of the water in which you are diving is also a factor. Salt water is denser than fresh water so you will need to carry more weight when diving in the ocean than in a lake.

Checking your weight

When using new equipment at a new location, every diver will need to do a weight check. Whatever system you use and however much weight you use, you should check that you are neutrally buoyant with a nearly empty tank and full equipment. Do this by checking that you float vertically with your eyes just above the surface with a full lung of air. Make sure that you sink under the water when you exhale fully.

How much lead should I use?

Many divers learn to dive with plenty of lead because it helps keep them on the bottom of the pool at a time when they may be nervous and breathing in large volumes of air. However, some divers will carry large amounts of ballast during routine dives. As a result, they never get to experience the joy of diving completely weightless, and they are always having to fin forward in order to stay at one depth. This means that they use a lot more air than they should. A relaxed diver has just the right amount of weight to complete the dive with a tank that is nearly empty.

INTEGRATED WEIGHT SYSTEMS

Some BCs have an integrated weight system. This is composed of two side pockets that have pouches (1), which contain the weights. These must be retained securely at all times until the moment when you want to release them. At this time, it should be easy to rip them away in order to either pass them up to a dive boat or jettison them in an emergency.

CYLINDERS, TANKS AND BOTTLES

A diver prepares **a range of cylinders** in different sizes, made of both steel and aluminum.

What's in a name?
Whatever you want to call them, cylinders, tanks or bottles are the transportable high-pressure vessels that contain the gas you are going to breathe. They can be made from steel or aluminum.

Steel or aluminum
Steel cylinders usually have a rounded bottom for weight-saving reasons, so they are fitted with a rubber base to allow them to stand upright. Aluminum cylinders,

because their metal is much lighter, can be made with a flat bottom.

Steel is much stronger than aluminum, so to add strength, an aluminum cylinder has much thicker walls and this can make them bigger. With less weight and more water displaced, using an aluminum tank means wearing more lead weight to compensate in the water. Often, aluminum cylinders of the same volume weigh more out of the water than a similar volume steel cylinder.

Full of air
The cylinder or tank has a valve screwed into the aperture at the neck. This is a cross-flow valve that works like a tap. You open it to let the gas out or close it to keep the gas in. There is a fitting that matches that of the regulator so that the regulator first-stage can be given an air-tight connection.

These cylinders are aluminum as shown by their flat bottoms. Because they are bigger, they weigh more at the surface and displace more water than steel cylinders.

COMMON CYLINDER SIZES
Tank sizes vary according to need. A normal leisure diver will probably be supplied by a dive center with an 80-cubic-foot (12-L) cylinder. Some women may prefer to carry a smaller, lighter 63-cubic-foot (10-L) cylinder. Larger men may prefer a bigger 105-cubic-foot (15-L) cylinder. A popular safety measure is to take a smaller cylinder strapped alongside the main cylinder—affectionately known as a "pony bottle."

These round-bottomed steel cylinders are twinned together with a gas manifold and have a smaller "pony" cylinder rigged alongside.

In the United States, tanks are measured by the volume of compressed gas in the tank, for example, 80 cubic feet. In Europe, Australia and New Zealand, tanks are measured by water capacity, for example, 12 L.

If you are in Europe, you can calculate the amount of gas in a tank if you know its internal volume and the pressure to which it has been filled. For example, a 12-L cylinder filled to 300 psi (200 bars) of pressure contains 2,400 L of gas. The pressure gauge of the regulator gives you an easily read figure and the internal volume, often calibrated as WC, is embossed on the outside wall of the tank, near its neck.

Some cylinders are routinely filled to 3,365 psi (232 bars) of pressure while others may even take 4,400 psi (300 bars) of pressure. The more gas that is squeezed into a tank, the longer it will last. The maximum working pressure (WP) is embossed on the outside of the tank together with a maximum test pressure (TP).

Because cylinders or tanks are filled to such high pressures, they need to be regularly tested in case of failure. A tank that fails under pressure would be lethal. In the U.S., a tank must have a hydro test every five years, and the date of this is stamped on the shoulder of the tank. The person who fills the tank will want to know it is safe to do so. Tanks are also visually inspected every year.

It's important to carry sufficient gas to complete the intended dive. This will depend on depth, the time needed to do the dive and the breathing rate of the diver.

The statutory period for **hydrostatic testing** varies from country to country. The neck is stamped with the expiry date of the test.

COMPRESSING GASES

Shipboard compressors are used in conjunction with an air bank of large cylinders so that demand can be met when needed.

Filling tanks

As we have seen, it is possible to compress a lot of gas into a small space. The total mass of the gas remains the same, but the molecules are pushed closely together. It is possible to fill a tank that would normally have, say, 0.4 cubic feet (12 L) of air at normal atmospheric pressure (1 atmosphere or bar) many times over so that eventually it might contain more than 200 atmospheres (200 bars).

Diving tanks are filled using a high-pressure compressor. First of all, a source of clean uncontaminated air is required. Positioning the compressor intake so that air does not get air contaminated with carbon monoxide or another unwanted gas is important, especially in an environment that may have a gas or diesel engine close by. This includes aboard boats, in urban areas or even close to the primary drive of the compressor.

For this reason, small, portable compressors are best used in windy locations. They have a long snorkel tube to the air intake that is as far away from the engine as possible.

The next problem encountered is that air expands when it gets hot, and the act of pressurizing air produces a lot of heat. Compressor designers get around this problem by compressing the gas in three or more separate stages, with

The latest **nitrox installations** use a low-pressure compressor (1) alongside the membrane de-nitrogenizing filters (2) and main compressor.

progressively higher pressure pistons and cylinders to each pump. This is called adiabatic compression. Between each stage, the air is transported through a long series of pipes equipped with heat exchangers. In bigger installations, these pipes are oil-cooled, but smaller compressors have big fans to cool the heat exchangers. Small air-cooled compressors need to be positioned so that they are in the shade and have a good flow of ambient air over them even if powered by electricity.

The act of compressing the air also squeezes any humidity out of it. This collects in the compressor in the form of a condensate, which is a mixture of condensation and oil vapor. Removal of this water is especially important when filling tanks with nitrox because the elevated levels of oxygen in

nitrox can combine with water and cause the inside of the tank to deteriorate.

The oil used in the compressor is special in that it is free of poisonous hydrocarbons. The air is also filtered both through carbon granules to remove any unwelcome flavor and through a molecular sieve to remove any unwanted content.

In order to compress air to make nitrox, it must be compressed twice. The latest installations have a low-pressure compressor installed alongside the main compressor in order to do this.

Big demand

No matter what the capacity of the compressor installation, there will always be fluctuation in demand, with everyone wanting to go diving at the same time. Most

commercial compressor installations bank the gas they compress into very large high-pressure cylinders so that it can be quickly decanted into the divers' cylinders when it is needed. This is especially common aboard dive vessels that use the time while cruising between dive sites to compress the gas for the next dive.

Small **gas–powered compressors** are best used in breezy locations to avoid contamination by the exhaust.

OTHER GADGETS

A round **surface marker buoy** is best for permanent surface use.

Dive shops are full of gadgets for divers but there are few that you will actually need. If you take too many unnecessary items with you on a dive, they will only hinder your progress rather than be of any use.

Buoys and reels

If you dive where the water is moving or need to mark your position for some other reason, use a surface marker buoy (SMB) at the end of a line. The line should be kept at the shortest length possible. A large, simple-to-use winder reel will help with this. Because there are so many bad reels on the market, some people prefer to use a simple spool instead.

Reels must have the ability to deploy, and wind back in, a sufficient length of line to do the job that's needed without tangling or jamming. There are many different devices available and you should be careful to choose a reel that has a spool made of one piece of material. A spool that breaks in two is worse than useless.

Some reels have easy-to-use ratchets but others are fiddly. Check that your chosen reel has metal parts that are of marine-grade 316 stainless steel. A large spool is less likely to jam than a smaller one but a smaller reel is

A **large reel** is less likely to jam and a sausage-shaped delayed deployment surface marker buoy is best.

more easily stowed and is, therefore, more likely to be there when you need it.

An SMB can be round or sausage-shaped. For permanent surface use, a round one tows behind the diver more easily.

Winder reels are often made mainly of plastic but any metal parts should be of marine-grade 316 stainless steel.

D-rings and undersuits

Many BCs are equipped with large stainless steel D-rings for clipping on items that are too big to stow securely in a pocket.

Something that is often forgotten when purchasing diving equipment is a suitable bag to put everything in. Bags come in a range of shapes and sizes, and it is important to have the right one.

Mesh bags are extremely useful. You can stuff your wet gear in one and then dunk the whole bag, loaded as it is, into fresh water to rinse it.

Regulator bags and briefcases are for carrying smaller, precious items.

Dive gear weighs a lot so a big bag is going to be heavy. Some divers manage to get everything in a backpack. An ordinary sports bag can be picked up by the handles and carried, but a heavy dive bag will need to be dragged and so wheels are essential. Once you've got wheels, you'll probably want an extending handle to help you maneuver your bag. Many divers prefer tough crate-style bags. Some bags combine a soft top with a plastic base.

One thing to bear in mind is that if you are flying, a heavy-duty bag of equipment alone can take up a great deal of your checked-in baggage allowance.

Many BCs are equipped with large **stainless steel D-rings** for clipping on larger accessories.

Undersuits

An undersuit is a very important accessory that is integral to the function of a drysuit. This high-tech item of clothing should have very good thermal properties but it must also take sweat away from the wearer's skin while at the same time repel any small quantities of water that might find their way onto the outer layer of the undersuit. Its insulating material must be exceedingly lightweight and yet allow air to circulate freely within it. An undersuit can be worn conveniently between dives, too, and they can be colorful.

A **thermal undersuit** is an important accessory for divers who use drysuits.

GASES AND PRESSURE

Understanding pressure

The molecules of gases are in free association and can be pushed closer together or remain farther apart depending upon the pressure put on them. Because of this, it is possible to compress thousands of cubic feet of air into a cylinder. The molecules of liquids do not behave in the same way, and it is not possible to squeeze a gallon of water into a pint glass.

It is essential that every diver understands the significance of **breathing gases under pressure**.

Boyle's Law

The first divers working inside large open-ended bells noticed that as the bell was lowered, the water level inside the bell rose, and it went up most in the first moments of descent. When the bell was brought up, the water level lowered, and the air seemed to

PRESSURE, VOLUME AND BUOYANCY

The relationship between pressure and volume has great importance to divers when it comes to buoyancy. Our own air spaces are fed with air from our regulators at ambient pressure but our wetsuits contain millions of tiny bubbles that get compressed as we go deeper making us feel apparently heavier. As we ascend this gas expands back and we feel lighter again.

magically return. It was the 17th-century scientist Robert Boyle who first explained this phenomenon. He formulated the mathematical relationship between gases and pressure. This formula is called Boyle's Law, and it states that the volume of a given mass of gas is inversely proportional to the pressure put upon it.

As divers, we can try this out for ourselves. If we take an open-ended bag or container down to 100 feet (30 m), where the pressure is 4 atmospheres (atm, 4 bars), and fill it a quarter full with air, the air will naturally want to make the bag rise. At 66 feet (20 m) and 3 atm (3 bars), we will see that the bag will be about one third-full of air. At 33 feet (10 m) deep and 2 atm (2 bars), the bag will be half full of air. At the surface, where pressure is 1 atm (1 bar), the bag will be completely full. You will notice that the greatest change occurs between 33 feet (10 m) and the surface.

Henry's Law

Something else important happens to gases and liquids while under pressure. Liquids tend to absorb gases and take them into solution until they are said to be "saturated" with gas. Your body acts like a liquid. At the surface, it is saturated with gas at 1 atm (1 bar) of atmospheric pressure.

The 19th-century American physicist William Henry investigated this phenomenon. Henry's Law explains that the amount of a gas that will dissolve into a liquid depends upon the pressure put upon it, and the absorption will continue until the liquid is saturated with the gas and can absorb no more. Henry's Law tells the diver that the greater the depth and the higher the pressure, the more gas the body will absorb.

Dalton's Law

A third important law is Dalton's Law of partial pressure, which was formulated by the English physicist John Dalton in 1801. His law states that each gas in a mixture creates pressure as if the other gases were not present. The total pressure is the sum of the

Depth	Pressure	Air volume
0 ft/0 m	1 atm/1 bar	Full
33 ft/10 m	2 atm/2 bars	1/2 full
66 ft/20 m	3 atm/3 bars	1/3 full
100 ft/30 m	4 atm/4 bars	1/4 full

The **compression effect** on gases due to depth is most apparent nearer the surface.

pressures created by the gases in the mixture. Air is a mixture of gases, mainly nitrogen and oxygen. The following pages will explain why this is important for divers.

> **TIP**
>
> UNDERSTANDING THE SCIENCE OF DIVING WILL HELP MAKE YOU A SAFER DIVER.

BREATHING COMPRESSED GAS

Easy breathing
When diving with scuba equipment, divers breathe compressed air that is delivered automatically, and cleverly, by the regulator or breathing valve at exactly the same pressure as the water surrounding them. This allows divers to breathe freely and without effort while underwater.

Breathing hazard
The hazard of breathing compressed air at depth is that if a diver were to hold a breath of compressed air and come up, the air held in the lungs would expand with the reducing pressure of the water, and do irreparable damage. The first rule of scuba diving is to continue breathing normally at all times and to never hold a breath.

Unfortunately, when first learning to dive, most people find their natural instinct is to hold their breath. This instinct is called the mammalian reflex. It is meant to prevent us from inhaling something that might kill us. Divers have to fight against this natural reaction; they have to get out of the habit of holding their breath, and instructors will keep emphasizing the point until their trainee divers get the message.

The greatest pressure changes and, therefore, the greatest volume changes happen near the surface. Even in shallow water, divers should never hold their breath while using scuba equipment.

Separate gases
Air is made up of two main gases. Oxygen makes up around 21 percent of air and the rest is mainly inert nitrogen.

Dalton's Law explains why the individual gases in a mixture of air must be considered separately. While some of the life-giving oxygen can be metabolized, the inert nitrogen is normally just breathed in and out, without being absorbed into the body.

Under pressure of the water, our bodies, which are mainly liquid, start to absorb some of the nitrogen in the air we breathe. It happens slowly at first, but as we go deeper or stay under longer, the effect is greater.

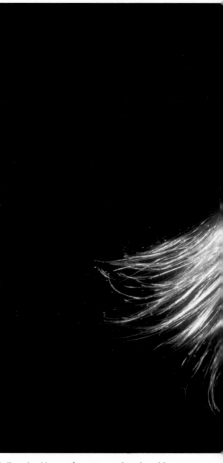

A diver should never forget to **continue breathing** normally at all times while using scuba equipment.

Decompression illness
Every time divers go under water, they absorb some nitrogen. At first this enters their blood, but with time, it is passed from the blood circulating around their bodies to other parts. As they go deeper and stay underwater longer, they absorb more nitrogen. On the ascent, the absorbed nitrogen passes back the other way, from the tissues to the blood and, via the lungs, out in the exhaled air.

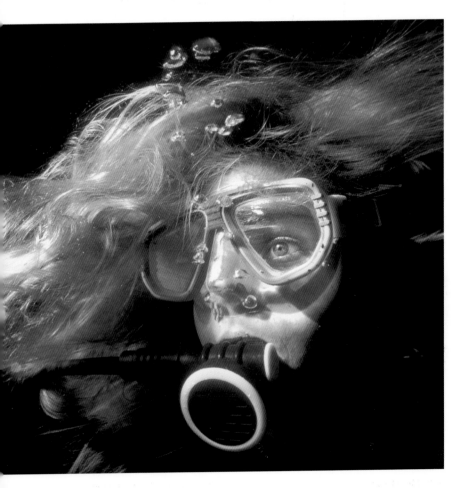

Divers must be sure to come up slowly to give their circulation time to complete this process, otherwise they can suffer the effects of decompression illness.

Decompression tables

Scientists like John Scott Haldane worked out the maximum times for different depths that were thought to be safe, and formulated them into tables. These are called no-stop times. If a diver goes to less than the maximum depth for less than the maximum time prescribed and comes up at a rate no faster than that prescribed by the tables, the body will not absorb more nitrogen from the air than it can safely release during the ascent and the diver will suffer no ill effects.

Divers must be careful to ascend the last few feet to the surface at the slowest rate possible to allow for the expansion of gas that was under pressure and the release of the nitrogen absorbed by the body.

> **TIP**
>
> ALWAYS ASCEND SLOWLY
> FROM EVERY DIVE.

SOUND AND LIGHT UNDERWATER

Hearing underwater

Our ears are designed to hear well in air. Sound vibrations travel through the air relatively slowly, and by using our two ears we can distinguish the direction that a sound comes from.

Water is about 800 times denser than air and sound vibrations travel around four times faster through this denser medium of water. The "silent world" beneath the sea is anything but that. It can be very noisy in the depths.

The problem underwater is that our ears can no longer distinguish the direction from which a sound is coming. Also, divers find that with the sound of inhalation, the noise coming from air passing through the regulator, and the gurgle of bubbles escaping, they can't hear anything else.

Light in the water

Light acts differently underwater, too. This is because light waves are refracted (bent) as they pass from one medium (such as air) to another (such as water). To reach our eyes, light underwater travels from the water into the pocket of air in our face masks. When it does this, it bends. As a result, things look one-third closer (or, some would say, one-third bigger) in the water than they do in air. Divers get used to it.

Color changes

Light is absorbed by water, which is why it gets dark in deep water. In turbid conditions, divers need a light to see by after only about 50 feet (15 m) of depth.

The color of light is selectively absorbed. Near the surface, the sunshine penetrates well and everything has a natural color. But within a few feet, red light is absorbed and things that are deep red appear to be black. Go deeper, and other colors are absorbed. Yellow light is lost by about 33 feet (10 m), and green light disappears soon after.

Of course, the color of objects is made up of a mixture of colors from the light spectrum so the color changes can be quite subtle at first. However, by around 66 feet

The **photographer's light** reveals the reef close up in all its vibrant colors.

(20 m) deep, everything starts to look a monochromatic blue because only the short, blue wavelengths of light can pass through the water easily.

If divers take a source of white light with them, such as a powerful diving light or a photographer's flashgun, they can hold it close to objects so that the light does not have to pass through more than a few feet of water. Then, the natural colors are restored. The effect can be startling. Fish and coral

With **daylight alone**, everything looks very blue at depth. The visibility in even really clear water is rarely more than 100 feet (30 m).

that looked a dull color are suddenly revealed in all their vibrancy. Pictures of coral reefs or wrecks are usually taken using powerful flashes of light with spectacular results.

Water clarity

The clearest water is still not usually very clear. It's full of plankton, tiny life forms that are the young of some sea creatures and the food of many animals, from tiny coral polyps to whales. There is also a lot of detritus. Everything is relative, though. If you could see for 100 feet (30 m) underwater, you would say that it was clear. However, if you could only see that far while driving your car, you would think it was very foggy indeed.

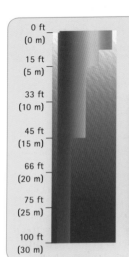

0 ft (0 m)	
15 ft (5 m)	
33 ft (10 m)	
45 ft (15 m)	
66 ft (20 m)	
75 ft (25 m)	
100 ft (30 m)	

COLOR ABSORPTION BY DEPTH
As light passes through water, it is progressively absorbed so that the environment not only becomes darker but also less colorful.

FLOATING AND SINKING

A properly equipped scuba diver can choose to be at any depth, neither floating nor sinking.

Understanding density

The Greek mathematician Archimedes discovered in the second century BC that when a body is immersed in a fluid, a force equal to the weight of the fluid displaced buoys the body up. This principle applies to both floating and submerged bodies and to all liquids and gases.

A fully equipped diver is made up of many constituent parts, some of which will naturally sink, such as the tank and weights, and others that tend to float, such as the suit buoyed up by the air contained within it.

A diver's body can either sink or float, depending on the amount of air in the lungs. The BC also has variable buoyancy. The equipped diver must be viewed as a whole, with the overall weight balanced against the amount of water displaced. This equals the overall density. Water has a different density depending on whether it is fresh or saltwater.

If the diver's overall density—complete with suit and equipment—is less than the density of the water, the diver will rise in the water column (float). If the diver's body and kit is denser than the water, the diver will sink in the water.

Adjusting buoyancy

The relative density of an object to the water also determines the proportion of a floating body that will be partly submerged in the water, as in the case of a diver with a BC inflated at the surface. For a submerged body, the apparent weight of the body is equal to its weight in air less the weight of an equal volume of water.

A diver has two ways to continually adjust his or her density. First, lung volume can be varied by altering the amount of air inhaled and exhaled. Second, the volume of air in the BC or drysuit can be adjusted.

A diver can become lighter than the water displaced by inflating the BC and floating at the surface. To sink, the diver can become heavier than the water displaced, and can do this quickly or slowly by altering the amount of air put into the BC.

When a diver gets to the depth required, sufficient air should be added so that the diver neither continues to sink nor floats up. This is called "neutral buoyancy." At this

BUOYANCY TEST

Do this simple buoyancy check when diving with unfamiliar equipment.

Float vertically at the surface with an almost empty tank and no air in the BC. If you are correctly weighted, you should float with your head well clear of the water when you have a full lung of air. When you exhale and empty your lungs, you should sink. A diver with perfect weighting for neutral buoyancy will float with their eyes above the surface when breathing normally. If you do this with a full tank, add extra lead (around 6 pounds or 3 kg) to compensate for the weight of the air you will use during the dive.

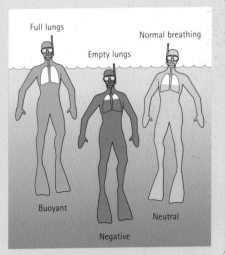

Full lungs

Normal breathing

Empty lungs

Buoyant

Neutral

Negative

point, little effort is needed by the diver to propel forward using a few fin strokes.

The art of diving depends on buoyancy control, and to be neutrally buoyant means that a diver becomes free and weightless in a liquid world.

Breath control

Of course, a diver is breathing in and out all the time. This means that their buoyancy changes slightly from moment to moment. But a diver doesn't have to keep fiddling with the direct-feed of air to the BC or drysuit to maintain buoyancy. It is easier to make fine adjustments to the buoyancy by simply altering lung volume. For example, taking a large breath will help a diver rise over an obstruction and a large breath out will help them to sink a little after passing it (*see also* pages 82–83).

Perfect buoyancy control allows a diver to hover midwater at will. Achieving neutral buoyancy is the essence of the art of diving.

WATER AND WEATHER

Waves can travel for miles across the ocean and arrive at places where the weather is otherwise calm.

Wind and waves

For divers, weather is about wind because wind causes waves. Inclement weather does not really affect the water once you are more than a few feet from the surface, but it certainly affects how you get there and how you get back. A sea that is flat calm today can be extremely rough tomorrow.

Waves are driven by the wind, but there doesn't need to be a big storm for the sea to have enormous waves. Waves are vibrations. A mighty storm in one area can cause the sea to vibrate, and these vibrations will travel for miles across the surface of the ocean. That is why, for example, the coasts off California and western England, South Africa and Australia enjoy good conditions for surfing but not always for traveling by small boat. Locations in the tropics are not always blessed with perfect conditions either. It can rain and be stormy even on an atoll in the Pacific Ocean.

A high surf can affect your ability to enter the water if you are diving from the shore, and it can make regaining the safety of a boat difficult and dangerous. Of course, a rolling sea also makes it more difficult for the crew to see you in the choppy water.

Using a forecast

You can anticipate what the sea will be doing by watching the weather forecast, but you will need to have an understanding of what the wind does.

Wind is created by currents of air moving from areas of high pressure to areas of lower pressure. A passing low-pressure weather system is usually accompanied by high winds and rain, and the weather front can be especially turbulent.

If a weather system is moving toward the coast, it will bring with it rough conditions. If it is moving away from the land, it may mean that although there are storms out at sea, the water close to the land is sheltered from the wind and so remains calm.

THE BEAUFORT SCALE

FORCE	SPEED (MPH)	DESCRIPTION	SURFACE CONDITIONS
0	0	Calm	Sea like a mirror.
1	1–3	Light air	Ripples with the appearance of scales are formed, but without crests.
2	4–7	Light breeze	Small wavelets, still short, but more pronounced. Crests have a waxy appearance and do not break.
3	8–12	Gentle breeze	Large wavelets. Crests begin to break. Foam of glassy appearance. Occasional white caps.
4	13–18	Moderate breeze	Small waves, becoming larger with white caps.
5	19–24	Fresh breeze	Moderate waves, taking a more pronounced long form; diving becomes marginal.
6	25–31	Strong breeze	Not suitable for safe diving.
7	32–38	Near gale	Not suitable for safe diving.
8	39–46	Gale	Not suitable for safe diving.
9	47–54	Severe gale	Not suitable for safe diving.
10	55–63	Storm	Not suitable for safe diving.
11	64–72	Violent storm	Not suitable for safe diving.
12	73–83	Hurricane	Not suitable for safe diving.

Sea breezes

There are other weather effects to consider. In the morning it may be calm, but as the land warms up in the sunshine of the day, hot air rises from it and cold air rushes in from the sea to replace it. This is why it tends to get windy in hot areas close to the coast. This is called a sea breeze and is an on-shore wind.

At night, the land cools down and the opposite effect happens: the wind blows off the shore. In the morning and the evening, there is a short period of calm weather when the temperature of the water and land are in equilibrium.

The Coriolis Effect

The rotation of the Earth causes the wind to swirl in massive weather systems. These weather systems are seasonally affected because as the planet travels around the sun, it tilts toward or away from it. As air moves from high to low pressure in the northern hemisphere, it is deflected to the right by the Coriolis Effect. In the southern hemisphere, it is deflected to the left.

In **warmer climates**, periods of calm usually occur during early morning and in the evening.

> **TIP**
>
> IT CAN SOMETIMES BE CALM CLOSE TO SHORE EVEN IF THERE ARE STORMS OUT AT SEA.

GAINING CONFIDENCE

You will soon **be confident** enough to take your regulator out of your mouth if you want to.

Practice, practice, practice

If you want to be good at anything, you need to practice. It's the same with scuba diving. All the skills you first learn in the pool, and later in open water, need to be practiced until you just do them without even thinking about it.

Accomplished divers—and you can easily become one of them—have no problem with taking their regulators out of their mouths and replacing them. They can clear water that may have found its way into their masks, clear their ears when they need to and adjust their buoyancy. It is second nature for them to manage their air supplies, know how deep they are and control their ascent. You will soon be able to do these things without giving them a second thought.

Once you are well practiced, you can manage yourself underwater as easily and confidently as you walk down the street!

Go diving

The only way to improve your skills and gain confidence is to go diving regularly. If you live far from the ocean, membership in a diving club will allow you to use a swimming pool for scuba diving on a regular basis. You can repeat your diving practice using all your equipment until your skills are honed to perfection

The first step is to manage your expectations. Once you have done that, your confidence will grow. For example, you may expect diving to be a claustrophobic experience, but then find yourself awed by the wide-open spaces encountered in the world below the ocean.

You may want to cling to your regulator in the mistaken belief that water will flood into your mouth when you take it out, but then be happy to find it does not. You'll soon gain the confidence to exhale in the knowledge that your regulator is always ready with another breath.

You may think that you will need to depend on others when you are diving, when in fact you will become the one that others can depend on.

Exercises to build confidence

A good exercise for improving confidence is to practice taking off your equipment in the pool and then replacing it. This will help you get to know where everything is. It's also good to take off your mask and swim around without it to build confidence.

Swimming blind with a mask blacked out with duct tape will give you the confidence to swim in conditions where visibility is poor. Going through your rescue skills and repeating them is essential practice. You never know when you may need them. Just spend time underwater to get used to the weightless conditions found there.

Having fun

Once you are able to manage yourself underwater, you can get on with enjoying being down there. Then, you can have fun looking at the marine life and even taking some photographs.

Once you are confident in your ability to conduct yourself underwater, you will be able to be more adventurous. One thrill of diving is getting close to the bigger undersea creatures. At first this may seem scary but these sea animals won't have any idea what you are and will only let you get so close before beating a hasty retreat.

This diver is **visiting the wreck** of the USS *Oriskany*, an obsolete aircraft carrier in Florida.

Eventually, you will find yourself doing things that your non-diving friends simply won't believe. You'll need to bring back plenty of photographs of yourself simply to ensure that they don't think you've become a fantasist!

You can have fun looking at the **marine life**. It's an entirely different world underwater.

GET READY TO DIVE

Divers get a good briefing from the dive guide so that they know what to expect before entering the water.

Poor preparation makes people perform poorly. Preparing yourself and your equipment properly before you leave the surface is the key to enjoying a dive.

What to expect

First, you need to know what to expect on the dive, and you can get that information from someone who's already done it. This means listening carefully to the dive briefing from the dive guide beforehand. If there is anything you do not understand, do not be afraid to question the expert on hand. The only stupid question is the one that you were afraid to ask.

You will need to know where you will enter the water and by what method (whether you'll be going by boat or entering the water from the shore); the depth at the entry point; and the maximum depth you are likely to encounter during the dive.

The dive guide will tell you about the prevailing current, which way you should swim and whether you should keep the reef or the wreck to the right or left. You'll be warned of any expected hazards and told how to deal with them. A good description of the dive site, complete with a sketch, will give you an idea of what to expect.

The purpose of a buddy check is to use a diving partner to ensure that everything is in place. It is a key safety issue.

Your guide will tell you the sort of animals to expect—although wild animals are unpredictable and may not make an appearance. You will be told the method by which you ascend and how you will be picked up by small boat. Alternatively, you may have to swim back to shore or to an anchored boat.

Checking equipment

The equipment you use should be appropriate to the dive, and it needs to be assembled and checked over to make sure all of it is working properly. Fit your regulator to the tank valve. Open the tank valve to check the pressure gauge. It shows how much air you have in your tank. Close the valve again and breathe the air that is in the hoses. When the gauge gets to zero, you won't be able to breathe in any more air. If it is still possible to breathe in, you've got a leak somewhere. If all is OK, open the tank valve fully immediately. Check the direct-feed hose

is attached properly to its connection on the BC, strap on your weights comfortably, and put on your tank and BC. Defog your mask before positioning it around your neck and locate your fins.

A buddy check

The purpose of a buddy check is to use a diving partner to ensure you have everything in place. Another advantage is that your buddy will become familiar with your exact equipment configuration, which may be different to their own.

The training agencies each suggest a different mnemonic to help develop a routine for this. One is BWRF. This stands for: Buoyancy (make sure the BC inflates and deflates properly); Weights (fit the weights securely); Releases (check where the releases to the buckles are); and Final OK. If all your equipment is well maintained and assembled correctly, there should be no problem.

Only once divers are fully briefed and have checked that all their equipment is rigged and functions properly are they **ready to dive**.

LOOK BEFORE YOU LEAP

Divers may often be asked to enter the water in a **synchronized moment** to ensure no one jumps on top of another diver that may already be in the water.

Staying safe is the first rule of scuba diving. It is more important than anything else.

Getting in

With all your predive checks completed, it's time to get into the water. Diving from the shore is simple. You just walk out through the shallows until it's deep enough to swim, then you can put your fins on. Things are different when diving from a boat or from a rocky shoreline.

Boat safety

The most dangerous thing you may meet when diving is your own boat. When you decide to leave the boat, you should get away from it as quickly and efficiently as possible. Boats have hard surfaces and rotating parts that are hazardous. Entering the water from bigger vessels is like jumping from a pier. Divers usually make a giant stride entry (see box on page 67) from these so that they get as clear from the hard edge of the platform as possible. The same entry method should be used to enter from a rocky shoreline next to deep water.

When **climbing the ladder** of a boat, keep your mask and regulator in place until you are safely on board.

Fins last

The last thing to do when getting ready to dive is put your fins on. A diver walking with fins is a hazard to himself or herself and to others, but a diver in the water without fins is unable to maneuver.

Put your fins on at the last moment and take them off as late as possible when leaving the water. To do this efficiently, go to the point of entry with your mask in place, and holding on firmly with one hand, use your other hand to put on your fins.

Jumping sense

The next thing to do is to make sure that the water is free of hazards before you jump in. Leaping on top of another diver who jumped in before you or who may even be coming up is potentially dangerous. It is very important to take a good look at the water before you jump in.

There will be occasions when there is enough space for more than one diver to make a giant stride entry at the same time. Each diver must be sure to enter his or her own patch of water without any danger of collision. A crash of divers loaded with heavy equipment could be serious. It is usually safest if all divers jump at the same time on a count of three, otherwise each should wait their turn, pausing while the previous diver swims clear.

Getting out again

You should never jump into the water without considering how you are going to get back out. Divers should also be very careful about the way they get out of the water because, again, it's the boat itself that represents the hazard.

Divers should be aware that although the boat may be at anchor, it is almost certain to be swinging gently in an arc through the water. This makes it slightly more difficult to grab hold of the ladder. Also, the boat may be moving up and down with the motion of the waves. If this is the case, it is best to get on to the ladder as the boat dips in the trough of a wave. To do this, step onto the ladder in one purposeful movement so that you are carried up with the boat's next rise on the wave.

Some dive ladders are designed for divers to climb out while they are fully equipped and still with their fins on. Other ladders require divers to take off their fins before climbing up the steps.

There should always be help on hand when divers are getting back on the boat. You should also keep your mask and regulator in place in case you fall back into the water.

GIANT STRIDE ENTRY

The giant stride entry is easy once you know how. With a little air in your BC and with your regulator firmly in your mouth, gather any loose equipment that might impact upon you when you hit the water. Holding your mask firmly in place with one hand, step out cleanly, making a giant stride as far as you can away from your starting point. Look straight ahead as you go. The air in your BC will bring you to the surface. Your mask will allow you to see because, by holding it in place, there will be no risk that it becomes dislodged on impact with the water. Give an OK signal to the person overseeing your entry if all is well.

TIP

YOUR BOAT MAY WELL BE THE
BIGGEST HAZARD YOU
ENCOUNTER WHILE DIVING.

Descending feet first, the diver constantly keeps a check on depth gauge or computer to monitor progress, and as a precaution against going deeper than planned.

That sinking feeling

To leave the surface of the water, you need to jettison all the air previously put in your BC because this air is causing you to float. If you are properly weighted, you will not sink on your own. You may need to perform a duck dive to push your body in a downward direction.

Duck diving

To duck dive, you should pivot at the hips to almost touch your toes, and then turn to move into an underwater handstand (although obviously your hands aren't standing on anything!). Pointing your legs with the fins straight up will cause them to protrude from the surface. At this time, their extra weight when no longer underwater should be enough to propel you downward and start you on your way.

Feet first

Descending feet first is often regarded as more sensible than duck diving, especially in conditions of poor visibility or if you are using a drysuit. You should keep an eye on the depth by watching the depth gauge or computer display so that there is no danger of going deeper than planned.

If there is a strong current, and it is important to reach a certain point on the reef (it usually is), it may be better to fin strongly downward headfirst, releasing any residual air that may be in the BC by pulling on a bottom dump valve.

Stay together!

It's very important that you do not lose sight of your buddy at this time or you may find yourself on the dive site without any company at all.

Sites with big currents

At dive sites that have big ocean currents swirling around small islands, you will find that the headfirst technique is needed. Such sites include the Maldives, Indonesia, the Cocos Island, and Papua New Guinea— all popular areas for diving. Often it is necessary to travel down at a 45-degree angle.

Descent lines

If you are diving at a very small site, such as a wreck, that location may be marked with a descent line attached to a buoy at the surface. The descent line is often held on the seabed by a large weight or anchor, or even tied to the seabed by the dive guide who descended first.

During a duck dive, the weight of the lower legs and fins unsupported by water will be enough to propel the diver downward.

You should be careful not to pull yourself down on the line. If it is held in place by a weight, it could be dislodged so that it drifts from the dive site. This can result in a dive in the wrong place for you and the divers who came down behind you. You will be less than popular with them!

The line should be used as a guide to mark the route to the right place. Run your hand down it by all means but try not to use it to aid your descent (you may be tempted to do this if you are a little too buoyant). Should you need to ascend prematurely for some reason (perhaps you had difficulty clearing your ears or you forgot something), the descent line also marks the quickest route back to where the crew of the boat will expect you to surface.

You can drop as fast as you like and as quickly as you are able to clear your ears. Many instructors suggest that you should not descend at speeds greater than about 100 feet (30 m) per minute for normal leisure dives but there is no real scientific reason for this.

Use a buoyed descent line as a guide but try not to pull on it or you may dislodge its ballast weight from the dive site.

COMING UP

Divers pause at between 20 feet (6 m) and 10 feet (3 m) aided by a reel of line attached to a buoy that was sent to the surface.

Going slow

You should always ascend slowly from a dive. This rule is as important as never holding your breath while scuba diving. Coming up in a controlled manner at the right ascent rate is essential to avoid decompression illness.

If you read and understood the section in this book on the science of scuba (see pages 52–59), you know that you should never hold your breath when ascending. The reducing pressure during the ascent causes the air in your lungs to expand, which is very dangerous.

The air that you put in your BC (or your drysuit) at depth will expand in the same way, just as will all the little bubbles of air in your wetsuit. This will make you progressively more buoyant and it could cause an uncontrolled runaway journey to the surface. To prevent this you must carefully release excess air by operating the dump valves provided. Your instructor will watch carefully to see that you do this during your training.

Releasing nitrogen

You should also remember that you will have absorbed inert nitrogen while you were underwater. You will need to give your circulatory system time to push that gas back out in the air you exhale.

Using diving computers

Today, almost every diver is equipped with a diving computer; your instructor certainly will be. These computers track your exposure to inert gases, as well as give you a readout of your ascent rate. There are visual and audible warnings if you exceed the maximum acceptable rate. As you know, pressure differences are greater as you near the surface. Most training agencies recommend that every diver stops between 20 feet (6 m) and 10 feet (3 m), and pauses there for between one and five minutes to decompress.

Types of ascent

Doing a free ascent—without a visual guide—needs complete buoyancy control. You need to be a competent diver and take extreme care to watch your instruments.

An easier way is to inflate a buoy on a line. The buoy goes up to the surface, and you gradually wind in the line on to your reel as you steadily ascend.

Another type of controlled ascent involves going back to the anchor line of the boat before you start your ascent and making your way up that. You will find a lot of divers prefer this because it leads directly to the boat, and it's easier to swim underwater than to ascend farther out and have to swim on the surface. You will still need to make your safety stop at around 20 feet (6 m) on the way up.

Whether you come up a line or make a free ascent, always remember to maintain neutral buoyancy by dumping excess air from your BC (or your drysuit). In that way, you can always ascend slowly from every dive.

A diver shows her **diving computer display** to her buddy during a slow ascent up the anchor line to their boat.

BUDDY DIVING

A diving instructor escorting a trainee diver is effectively diving alone.

Spare air
Divers learn early on in their training how to share air with another diver. Most divers carry an "octopus rig"—a spare regulator enabling them to share air with their buddy if necessary. If a pony bottle is carried, then a separate air supply is available.

Diving with a buddy
Every training agency dictates that divers should dive in pairs, and the person with you is usually known as a buddy. Diving agencies recommend diving with a buddy so that there is help at hand in an emergency.

However, diving with a buddy is no excuse to be sloppy about your preparation or the way you conduct yourself underwater. All divers should be trained to be totally competent and able to rescue themselves if something should go wrong. You should not think that you have a buddy because you are going to need one—but rather that your buddy may need you.

Is a buddy essential?
When you are learning to dive, you usually feel confident that nothing will go wrong because you have an instructor close by. But who will come to your instructor's aid if things go wrong? Your diving instructor must know how to get out of tricky situations without help.

SOLO DIVING

Solo diving is a controversial subject because training agencies recommend diving in pairs. However, diving professionals often dive alone, including an instructor escorting a solitary trainee or a diver who swims down to tie a mooring line to a wreck. An underwater photographer who spends the dive looking through the camera is effectively diving alone even if a buddy is present. As underwater photography becomes more popular, many leisure divers are putting themselves at risk. You should never undertake any such activity unless you are fully competent at self-rescue.

In most cases, during the early stages of your training, a dive master or an assistant instructor will help the instructor. Later, you may find yourself diving with an instructor or a dive guide and no one else. In this situation, the instructor or dive guide is effectively diving alone. To become a truly competent diver, you must learn (as your instructor has) how to cope if something goes wrong when you are on your own and you cannot rely on your buddy.

Why dive with a buddy?

It's good to dive with a partner because it makes sense to have someone to discuss the dive with before you descend into deep water. Dives should always be planned carefully, and any defects in the dive plan need to be identified and corrected. There is a greater chance of spotting any potential difficulties if there are two divers to go over the plans.

It's sensible to have someone else look over your equipment and point out any problems in the way you have rigged it. It's also useful to have someone to help you put on your equipment. A buddy check enables your partner to become familiar with your gear. This is especially important if your equipment is not the same. In a similar way, you can become familiar with your buddy's equipment.

Once you are underwater, you will see and experience many fantastic things. There is something wonderful about sharing this exclusive world with another person, and many good friendships form between buddies. It's great to have company, and when you return from a dive, you will have someone with whom to share the memory.

Two's company. It is great to share an underwater experience with another person and you'll have lots to talk about with them afterward.

BREATHING

How long will a tank last?

The big question that every new diver asks is: how long will the air in my tank last? The answer depends on how much air there is in the tank to begin with, at what depth it is going to be breathed in and how much air the diver is going to breathe.

In the United States, tank capacity is measured in cubic feet. An 80 cubic-foot tank has 80 cubic feet of air in it at 3,000 psi (if it is an aluminum tank). It is best to set aside a reserve of air, and conventional thinking suggests that one-quarter of the initial supply be kept aside. This may be overcautious with a large tank, but divers have to make a judgment based on the circumstances they expect to encounter. Let's assume that our 80 cubic-foot tank has only 60 cubic feet of air at our disposal with the rest held in reserve.

The next thing to identify is the depth at which the air is going to be breathed. At 100 feet (30 m) deep, the regulator delivers air at four times the pressure that it would at the surface. Thus, if we are diving at this depth, we have only 15 cubic feet of air to breathe (60 divided by 4).

How much air do you need?

The amount of air you need depends on several factors. Body size is important—a slender woman with small lungs will probably

The duration of **a diver's air supply** is dependent upon the depth it is breathed at and the amount of energy demanded by the work load.

breathe a lot less than a heavy-weight boxer, who will have large lungs to pump a huge amount of air. Activity and stress are also important. A relaxed man may breathe only 0.3 cubic feet (8 L) every minute, but increase his heart rate by increasing his workload or stress him in some way and this can leap to 1 cubic foot (30 L) per minute.

Fitness is not necessarily an indication of breathing rate. An older diver who has smoked all his life may not be very fit, but if he is relaxed—and often that comes with experience—he will use less gas than a young trained athlete who is working hard underwater. If you have to swim, you will consume more than if you are merely hovering in the water. Even thinking uses a lot of energy.

Training agency manuals usually use a figure of 0.9 cubic feet (25 L) per minute in their examples of how to calculate air consumption. At 100 feet (30 m), an 80 cubic-foot tank (with 20 cubic feet held in reserve) would last only 16 minutes (60 divided by 0.9 divided by 4).

Breathing underwater

Potential divers all want to know how it feels to breathe from a regulator underwater. It feels exactly the same underwater as it does if you try it on land in a dive shop. Either underwater or on land, you breathe in as there is a faint resistance as the valve pulls open. The mouthpiece floods with air that you inhale. It stops when you stop. When you exhale, there is slight resistance as the exhaust valve opens to allow the air to escape. The exhaled air then bubbles away.

CALCULATING YOUR AIR REQUIREMENT

The amount of air in the tank is divided by the respiratory mean volume or breathing rate multiplied by the absolute pressure in bars at the depth at which it is breathed.

You may know how much air is in your tank, but you need to keep a reserve because your own breathing rate is affected by many variables.

CLEARING YOUR EARS

A diver **pinches her nose** to aid in clearing her ears while descending.

Ear problems

Many people say that they cannot learn to dive because they get pain in their ears when they swim underwater. This is not surprising because if you don't know how to clear your ears, whether you're scuba diving or simply swimming underwater, you will be in danger of rupturing an eardrum—a very painful experience!

How the ear works

Ears have an outer section—the part we can see consists of a fleshy flap called the pinna, which gathers sound, and a hole that leads to the eardrum. The eardrum is exactly that— a membrane of tightly stretched tissue like a drum. This tissue vibrates as it contacts sound waves that move through the air.

The vibrations are transmitted via a set of tiny bones to a vibration sensitive window in the cochlea—the complex organ that holds the aural nerve and forms the inner ear.

The inner ear also contains semicircular canals filled with fluid that enable us to recognize how our body is positioned, whether horizontal or vertical.

The part between the outer ear and the inner ear is known as the middle ear. It is normally full of air at the same pressure as the air around us. It is connected to the throat by the Eustachian tube, but to stop any liquid from entering our ears when we drink, the Eustachian tube has a constriction at its lower end.

Water pressure

When you go underwater, water enters the outer ear cavities and presses on the eardrums—you can feel this pressure.

Because the air on the other side of the eardrum is at the pressure it was when you breathed in before your dive, there is an imbalance and the eardrums are distorted. You need to redress this balance before the pain becomes intense and the eardrums rupture.

A diver breathes air from a regulator at the same pressure as the surrounding water. But this air doesn't enter the middle ear from the mouth via the Eustachian tube because of the constriction in the tube.

To clear the constriction, pinch your nose and blow gently. You will force air at the same pressure as the water past the constriction and into the middle ear. You will hear your ears "pop" and the discomfort will pass immediately.

The important thing is getting the inhaled air past the constriction. Some people can do that by wiggling their jaw or simply by swallowing to open the constriction momentarily.

As long as your Eustachian tube is not blocked—perhaps because you have a head cold—pinching your nose and blowing gently against the pinch should always clear your ears without difficulty.

Make it a habit

Divers usually clear their ears without giving it a second thought. It becomes a natural thing to do. You should do it the moment you are aware of the pressure and long before there is any pain.

Going up and down

On the ascent, the air in the Eustachian tubes expands and forces its way past the constriction, just as any fluid in your middle ear drains naturally into your throat cavity. You shouldn't notice anything.

On the way down to a dive, you should never continue to descend if your ears hurt. If that happens, go shallower and try again.

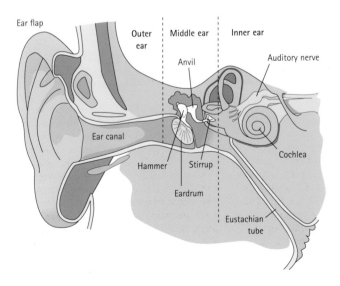

Ear flap

Outer ear · Middle ear · Inner ear

Anvil

Auditory nerve

Ear canal

Cochlea

Hammer · Stirrup

Eardrum

Eustachian tube

The eardrum effectively separates the inner ear from the outside world. While this plays a vital role in hearing, it can prove problematic when entering the high-pressure world of scuba diving.

CLEARING A MASK AND MOUTHPIECE

Wearing a mask

You should never strap a mask so tightly to your head that the frame distorts. Doing so will cause the mask to sit uncomfortably on your face, and it will be more likely to let water inside. The water pressure should be enough to maintain the watertight seal. The strap is simply meant to keep the mask in place on your head.

You can **clear water** out of your mask by exhaling air through your nose.

Clearing your mask

If you are diving deep in the ocean and your mask is dislodged and floods with water, you need know how to clear your mask.

A diving mask always includes a pocket that encloses the nose. This pocket gives you access to your nose so that you can pinch it to clear your ears, but it also allows you to eject water from a flooded mask.

To clear the water from your mask, hold the mask firmly against your head so that the skirt makes a good seal. Tilt your head back so that the water is all at the bottom of the mask and exhale gently through your nose. It's a bit like blowing your nose without a handkerchief.

The air that is blown from your nose into the pocket formed by your mask pushes the water out through the bottom of the skirt where the mask is not held so firmly in place. The interior of your mask is no longer full of water but is now full of air.

You will find that small amounts of water will enter your mask from time to time when you are underwater. Holding the top rim of the mask frame and exhaling slightly through your nose is usually all it takes to keep your eyes and your mask dry.

Mask clearing is one of those skills that should be practiced until you can do it as easily as blowing your nose. Once you have mastered this technique, you should be able to take your mask off underwater and replace it again or even change your mask for another one.

Clearing your mouthpiece

If you periodically take your mouthpiece out of your mouth while submerged, you won't drown but the interior of the regulator will flood with water.

As long as you exhale first when putting the mouthpiece back in, the water in the mouthpiece will be pushed with the exhaled air through the exhaust port of the regulator.

Sometimes, you may find that you have just breathed out when you dropped your regulator. What happens then?

All regulators have a purge control at the front. When this is pushed, it releases a strong yet progressive flow of air from the tank. This pushes out any water that may still be inside the second-stage of the regulator.

Essential advice

Whenever you do not have a regulator in your mouth, make sure your airway is open by exhaling some air gently from your mouth. It is also a good idea to do this when ascending to allow some of the air that your body has absorbed underwater (and that is slowly expanding on the ascent) to escape through your mouth.

Taking your regulator out of your mouth while underwater presents no problem. Just remember to **keep your airway open** by gently exhaling while you are doing it.

FINNING SKILLS

Going nowhere?
Some divers find that even though they bought the latest high-tech fins, they are not making the progress through the water that they would like. They see others in cheap old flippers shooting past them. They have difficulty swimming into the tiniest bit of current and often find they use up a lot of air and are exhausted after a swim.

To make swimming less of an effort and more efficient, you need to know how to use your fins properly. Your scuba instructor will help you to do that.

Getting it right
A pair of fins fitted to your feet gives you the opportunity to use the most powerful muscles in your body—your thigh muscles. If you just make bicycle movements with your legs to move around in the water, you won't make much forward progress. You need to be sure to present the blade of each fin at the best angle to the water in order to shift as much water as you can and propel yourself forward.

An efficient scuba diver does not use his or her arms when swimming. Instead the **powerful thigh muscles** are called into play.

Finning practice
This exercise can be practiced in the pool with your fins on. Face a wall and stretch out your arms so that your hands or fingertips touch the pool wall. Point your feet and stretch your legs out rather like a ballet dancer. Now, lift one straightened leg and kick downward, then do the same with the other leg. Repeat the movement with the first leg and keep going. You should be able to feel the force that you are creating with your legs as your hands are pushed into the pool wall.

Finning efficiency
The downward kick has the most effect in pushing you through the water. It doesn't matter if you bend your knee a little on the backward stroke. Just keep kicking.

You'll find that you can take long leisurely fin strokes and enjoy good results. You don't have to flutter kick very fast unless you are using a special pair of fins designed for you to do that. The long, leisurely fin strokes are so effortless that you will find that you can keep them up for a long time and travel a considerable distance.

The efficiency of this stroke means that if you find that you turn a corner of the reef and encounter a fierce current, you will have plenty of energy in reserve to fin quickly and accelerate through it to where the water is calm again.

Being efficient with your fins, and using the most powerful muscles you've got, means that you will exert less effort and use less air when swimming.

The **downward kick** has the most force.

Arms to the sides

The hands of scuba divers are used for grasping and holding things. Do not use them to do the breaststroke, instead put them down by your side or fold them across your chest. Any sudden arm movements can be a nuisance and even catch in the regulator hose of another diver, perhaps pulling out the mouthpiece.

Once you've got your finning action right, it's time to look at the rest of your gear. Make it as streamlined as possible. A diver should swim horizontally. If you tend to walk upright through the water, you probably need to check your buoyancy control.

If you use your fins correctly, you will be able to **swim long distances** in exchange for very little effort.

> **TIP**
>
> THE DOWNWARD KICK IS THE MOST EFFECTIVE IN PROPELLING YOU FORWARD.

BUOYANCY CONTROL

Underwater photographers need to have perfect buoyancy control so that they do not accidentally collide with the reef.

Perfect weightlessness

The art of diving is to achieve perfect weightlessness. This means having control of your buoyancy—to be neither floating up nor sinking down and to be able to go in any direction at will, with the least effort. This is what scuba diving is all about. It is called neutral buoyancy.

To achieve this, you need to get your weights right. They should be correct for your equipment and the suit you are wearing, as well as the water you are diving in.

Balancing your weight

The ideal weight that you should aim for in a particular body of water is enough to allow you to float vertically with your eyes just above the surface. This should happen when you are wearing a full tank and your lungs are full of air.

When you are floating in this way, you should begin to sink if you exhale. Inhaling from your regulator should make you rise back to where you were. You should never drop like a stone. This simple test takes into account the weight of air you will consume

during the dive. At the end of a dive, with your tank empty, you will find that breathing in a lungful of air will raise your chin and shoulders well clear of the water's surface.

Keep your weight down

By having the minimum amount of lead weight as ballast, you will need the minimum quantity of air in your BC or suit.

Some divers believe that wearing plenty of weight isn't a problem because you can always add more air to your BC or suit to compensate for it. While this may be true, it makes achieving true neutral buoyancy much more difficult.

As you go deeper and rise up again, the air in your BC or suit is subject to ever-changing compression and expansion. Therefore, the amount of water the air displaces is forever changing. If you put a lot of air in your drysuit, it will move around, causing you to move with it. You will find that you have to make constant corrections by injecting and dumping air.

Going up

Many inexperienced divers can be seen swimming in a semi-upright position through the water. This is because they have either too much lead or not enough air in their BCs.

They are swimming upright because a lot of their effort in finning is used to maintain their depth rather than to progress in a horizontal direction.

If your buoyancy is almost correct and you try to swim in a semi-upright position, you will head in the direction you are pointing to, which is up. As you rise, the air in your BC will expand. When this happens,

you risk embarking on an unplanned buoyant ascent to the surface.

The rule for good buoyancy control is use the minimum amount of lead combined with the minimum of buoyancy-compensating air.

In neutral

Neutral buoyancy means that all the effort you put into finning will go toward moving you in a horizontal direction. If you can achieve this, your air consumption will be dramatically reduced.

Once your buoyancy control has been perfected, it allows you to enjoy your dive and experience the underwater world around you. It also frees you to pursue your interests. For example, you can take closeup photographs of a reef without the risk of accidentally crashing into it—and potentially damaging its delicate structure—because you are not in control of your buoyancy.

> **TIP**
>
> MAKE INSTANT ADJUSTMENTS TO YOUR BUOYANCY BY VARYING THE AMOUNT YOU BREATHE IN AND OUT.

The art of diving is to achieve **perfect weightlessness**, neither sinking down nor floating up.

EQUIPMENT FAILURE

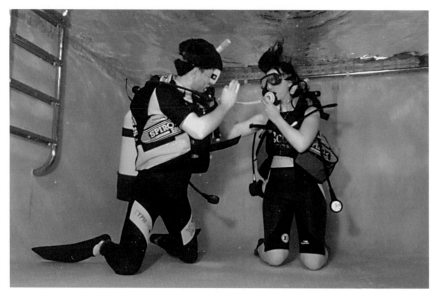

There are very few incidents of equipment failing underwater, but it's sensible to consider what can go wrong. If you do experience a problem, your training should mean you take it in stride.

A broken mask

If your mask is continuously flooding, either the seal of the skirt is damaged or the frame is broken. If this happens to you on a dive, you just have to clear your mask as often as needed until you reach the surface. To avoid this situation, some divers carry a spare mask in a BC pocket.

Regulator failure

Regulators rarely fail, but it is possible. Sometimes, a hose has become old and brittle and breaks, gushing air. If this happens, you should use your buddy's alternate air source until you can get to the surface. Otherwise, make a free ascent, keeping your airway open all the way.

Breathing from a **free-flowing regulator** is easy if you have practiced somewhere safe beforehand.

Practice using **an alternate air source** by sharing air with your buddy in sheltered water like a pool.

If your regulator has developed a small hole in the mouthpiece and is letting in water, it will make your breathing damp but you'll probably be able to finish the dive. If not, pull off the mouthpiece and insert the metal or plastic stump directly into your mouth.

Faulty tank O-rings tend to blow when they have the most pressure on them, either before or early in the dive. If this happens, you will usually have time to abort the dive.

If you are diving in cold, fresh water and your regulator starts to free-flow uncontrollably, you should continue breathing from it but allow the excess air to escape harmlessly into the water. You should abort the dive immediately. It is sensible to practice what to do in this situation in the controlled conditions of a swimming pool.

Some divers carry a separate **pony cylinder** and regulator as an emergency backup.

Other problems

If the dump valve on your BC sticks open, you have a serious problem and should abort the dive immediately by swimming to the surface. You should be able to do this easily if you are not carrying too much lead.

If you lose your weightbelt, you will start a buoyant ascent immediately. To slow yourself down, lie horizontally and flare your arms and legs. Keep your airway open, shouting "Arghhhh!" if need be.

A leak in your drysuit means you will get cold, but your BC will help maintain your buoyancy. Contrary to popular belief, a flooded drysuit weighs nothing underwater. However, it does make climbing a boat ladder difficult because of the weight of water in it.

Should your computer fail to work, stay close to and slightly shallower than your buddy. Never go deeper than your buddy. You can use your buddy's computer to help you get safely to the surface. Many divers now carry a second backup computer that will be up to date with their decompression status, ready for the next dive.

Another potential problem is if the camband of your tank is not sufficiently tight. If this happens, show your buddy that

it is dropping out so that your partner can push it back and tighten the strap.

If your buddy runs out of air, offer them an alternate air source and abort the dive. Obviously, if you run out of air, your buddy should do the same for you. It is important to practice sharing an alternate air source in a swimming pool.

Some divers carry a spare 16-cubic-foot (3 L) cylinder of air with its own independent regulator. This is often known as a pony.

It is vital to be well practiced in your rescue skills so that you will be able to cope with any emergency.

Some divers carry **two independent cylinders** on their backs, each with its own regulator, to provide additional safety.

AIR-SHARING

Once the out-of-air diver is settled, both divers should **abort the dive** and, taking a tight grip on each other, head for the surface.

In the early days of scuba diving, people practiced sharing one regulator between two people. This was easy to perform in the pool but was probably responsible for a lot of accidents in the sea.

The octopus rig
Someone then realized it made sense to fit an alternate second-stage to the regulator, called the octopus rig.

Every diver should be equipped with an alternate air source for use by another diver. Training agencies have different suggestions on how to do this. Some suggest you rig your

octopus to the right so that it is on the same side as your primary regulator. However, this can prove awkward for another diver to breathe from. Other agencies tell you to rig it on the opposite side so that another diver can access it more easily. Some agencies

An **octopus rig** on a standard hose hung from the right-hand side can prove awkward to use by another diver.

suggest that a diver should have the secondary regulator on a long hose so that it is good for sharing. This means stowing it under an elastic strap at the side of the tank. Other agencies insist that the primary regulator is on a long hose looped under the arm and over the shoulder so that another diver can take it in an emergency. The secondary regulator is rigged on a necklace for the first diver to use.

Yet another way is to have an alternate second-stage combined with the direct-feed to the BC. This can only be used by the wearer of the BC, so the primary regulator must be given to the other diver.

Whatever way you rig your alternate air source, it should be clearly visible so your buddy can find it easily.

Why share?
Diving equipment is simple and reliable and rarely fails underwater. The main reason that someone may need to share the air of another diver is because they mismanaged their air supply. Consequently, the only time you are likely to need to share is in the shallows when it may be necessary to do an unplanned decompression stop. Otherwise, it makes more sense to swim up to the surface.

It is important to start a dive with an air supply that is sufficient to complete a dive as planned. This means having a good idea of

An **alternate second-stage** combined with the direct-feed control of a BC.

what your air requirements are. On the dive, you should look at your pressure gauge and manage the supply. With a 50-bar reserve, it should never be necessary to share air. If you manage your own supply too finely, you could have problems should another diver, who is probably distressed and breathing heavily, wants to use some of the air that remains in your tank.

In the unlikely event that someone will need air, get them breathing from your alternate air source by offering it to them with the purge slightly depressed so that it is bubbling and will not need clearing. They may not be capable of blowing into it to clear the mouthpiece. Or they may not know where the purge button is. Start heading toward the surface immediately at a safe ascent rate. You can blow orally into a BC corrugated hose to provide buoyant support at the surface if needed.

Wherever you rig your alternate second-stage or octopus rig, it should be clearly visible and **easy to deploy** when required.

SIGNS AND SIGNALS

You can't talk underwater unless you and the person you want to talk to have expensive communications systems.

Expensive **underwater communications systems** for leisure divers have not proven very popular even though they allow divers to have conversations underwater.

Sign language

Normally, you will have to use signs and signals to communicate. Unless you and your buddy are proficient in sign language, it's best to keep these signals very simple.

Divers use an international code of simple hand signals. This has the advantage that if you are diving with someone who speaks a different language than you, you can still understand each other underwater.

Direction is indicated with the thumb. The up direction is indicated by a thumbs up, and down by a thumbs down. This can cause a little confusion at the beginning when newly trained divers use the thumbs up to say they are OK. The OK signal is made by placing the thumb and index finger tip to tip to create an "O" with the other fingers straight. It can be used as both a question and an answer.

To show another diver that you are near to using your reserve of air, make a fist and hold it up palm side toward the viewer. The emergency signal that you are out of air

The **OK sign** is given both as a question and an answer.

The thumb is used to indicate the intended **direction of travel,** either up or down.

is a chopping motion with the side of the flattened hand against the throat.

If you have a problem—with your ears, for example—point to the source of the problem with one hand using an outstretched index finger and flutter the other hand.

Go over your signals

It is important to go through the signals you intend to use with your buddy during your buddy check to avoid any misunderstandings. For example, making a T-shape with the tips of the outstretched fingers pointing to the center of the horizontal palm of other hand seems to have lots of different meanings. These include a request for "time out" or a signal that you are halfway through your air supply.

Dive guides use all sorts of signs to indicate different animals they are trying to draw your attention to. During the predive briefing, ask for a demonstration of the signs the dive guide intends to use.

Complex messages can be relayed between divers by writing with a soft pencil on a plastic slate. Divers can often be seen with these large rectangles of white plastic attached to them by a lanyard. It is important to keep the message simple and to write legibly in large letters.

People have devised many ingenious signals using a lamp in the dark. The boat crews may use their lights to signal Morse code to each other. However, it's best to stick with the signals you know, shining the light on your hand so that the signal is clearly lit.

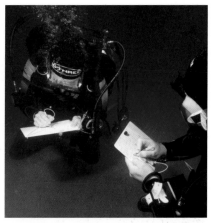

Divers can communicate more complex messages to each other by writing with pencils on **plastic diver's slates**.

A continuously revving engine or the noise of someone hammering on the hull or the boat's ladder are commonly used to signal from a boat to the divers below that they should return immediately. This is a good method, as sound travels very well in the dense medium of water.

> **TIP**
>
> ASK FOR A DEMONSTRATION OF THE SIGNS THE DIVE GUIDE INTENDS TO USE.

This signal means **"on my reserve supply."**

This chopping motion signals **"out of air."**

Any **other problems** are indicated by pointing and fluttering the other hand.

FINDING YOUR WAY

One diver **navigates with the compass** while the other operates the winder reel for the surface marker buoy (SMB).

The primary method of navigation underwater is simply to know where you are going and where you have come from. This allows you to retrace your route if need be.

Be observant

You should always take note of your surroundings and look at the view behind you so that you know what the return journey will look like. If you keep the reef or wreck on your left on the outward trip, you just keep it on your right for the return journey. But you will still need to know what the terrain looks like where you first entered if you are to ascend in the same place. It's a good idea to make a mental note of prominent parts of the topography or wreck site.

The position of the sun together with the position of underwater topography and visible features help a diver to know a return route.

Getting lost underwater happens a lot less often than you may think. This is because divers have an important source of information about their whereabouts—their depth.

Divers in the ocean navigate in a three-dimensional space, and if you know where you are in relation to the surface you can always reach it. If the seabed is getting shallower, you are probably heading toward a shore or the top of a reef. The ripple marks in a sandy seabed reveal the angle at which the waves are hitting the beach.

You should make a note of where the sun is. Its light may be refracted through the water, but it is usually possible to tell if it is behind you or to one side.

Compasses

Compasses are useful navigational tools, but you need to be confident in your ability to read and hold a compass properly.

A compass needle always swings to the north if it is free to do so. You must be careful to hold the compass level so that the needle can rotate freely. A compass is magnetic, so large areas of ferrous metal will affect it. For this reason, a compass is useless on a steel wreck. It may also be affected near a steel tank. A simple underwater magnetic compass is a useful tool as long as you are aware of its limitations. There are also some sophisticated electronic compasses available.

Competent use of a **compass** should allow you to swim away from a point and return to it with relative ease.

READING A COMPASS

To use a compass properly, you need to hold it so that the white arrow along the body of the compass is pointing in the direction you want to travel. Always ensure that the compass needle is allowed to swing freely. Rotate the bezel so that the position of the compass needle is marked. Adjust your direction as you swim so that the needle remains in the same place. When it is time to return, rotate the bezel with its marker through 180 degrees. Remember to stop when you get to where you want to be. Some compasses have a sight glass that allows you to read off a bearing.

Navigational methods

One method you can use to make sure you end up where you started is to divide your journey into three segments of equal length. By turning through 90 degrees at the end of each segment, you should end up near to where you started.

To navigate around a wreck, especially in poor visibility, you can use the line you used to descend to reach the wreck. Take a line and winder reel and clip the line of the reel to the line you descended. You then let it unwind, tying it off occasionally to handy points on the wreck. When it's time to return, you just wind the line back in until you reach what has now become your line up to the surface.

Use **a winder reel and line** on a wreck. Tie off the line to handy points as you progress so that it safely marks the route back.

PRACTICE MAKES PERFECT

Remember to keep
your airway open
when removing and
purging a regulator.

You should practice basic safety drills, such as clearing your mask and regulator mouthpiece, whenever you can. Both are essential skills, and a swimming pool is the ideal place to practice them. If you are a member of a diving club, there are usually pool sessions once a week.

Mask removal
Removing and replacing a mask successfully underwater is one of the most difficult tasks that a new diver has to learn. There seems to be a psychological barrier to overcome, which is probably a result of the mammalian reflex that tells you to hold your breath when you feel water on your face.

The trick is to do it in easy stages. Start by lifting the skirt of your mask to let a little water in and then blow the water out with air from your nose. When you are confident with that stage, try half-filling your mask and clearing it (see also pages 78–79).

Do not remove your mask underwater until you know you can clear it easily and even then, for the first attempts, try submerging from the surface with your mask in your hand rather than taking it off when fully immersed.

Eventually, you will be able to take your mask off completely and swim around the pool, breathing with your regulator. You will be amazed how competent you become.

Useful exercises
The swimming pool is the ideal environment in which to practice swimming with neutral buoyancy because it is more difficult to do in

Become competent at flooding and clearing a mask in the pool by progressing in easy stages.

Your instructor will demonstrate how to do **fin pivots** in the quest for good buoyancy control (above). The pool is also a great place to **practice removing equipment** and putting it back on again (right).

shallow water. You will have been taught during your first wet lessons how to do fin pivots.

Time underwater in the pool allows you to become totally familiar with your equipment. It is worth experimenting with different ways of rigging it. You can practice taking it off and getting it all back in place while you are still submerged. This may not have any practical application when you are diving but it helps build your confidence.

Another good exercise is to try breathing from a free-flowing regulator. You do this by tilting your head to one side to allow excess air to escape and pushing the purge button fully to simulate an uncontrolled flow of air.

Emergency ascents

Practice emergency swimming ascents by swimming horizontally, one arm outstretched, while you exhale from your mouth all the way. Make sure you keep your regulator in your mouth in case you get it wrong! A simulated swimming ascent is best done horizontally because it removes the hazard of pressure changes as you go up. Remember to never hold your breath while breathing compressed gases.

You should wear a thin wetsuit when you practice. It will give you a more accurate idea of what it will be like on a dive. If you practice in a new drysuit in a warm pool, be aware of the problem of overheating.

You should be careful how you handle your equipment in a swimming pool, especially when getting into the water and out again. Always use the ladder and never walk around poolside while wearing your fins. Make sure that there is a responsible person with rescue skills supervising your pool sessions.

Practice **emergency swimming ascents** by swimming horizontally in the pool.

SMALL-BOAT DIVING

Inflatable boats can take heavy loads but tend to be cramped. Divers may travel fully equipped to the dive site if it is only a short distance and the sea is calm.

Going by boat

Most divers soon get tired of having to swim out from the shore. Usually, a boat takes the divers to the dive site.

Sometimes the boat is quite small, either because the distance is not very great or because a small boat is being used in conjunction with a larger vessel that would not be safe to bring up close to a reef. When divers are picked up after a dive, it makes much more sense to use a small, maneuverable boat, some of which are extremely fast.

Divers may travel the short distance in a small boat wearing all their equipment, with tank and fins in place. However, you should

not try to get into a small boat from a jetty or a larger vessel with your fins on. You should pass them down before stepping in when the operator tells you to. Try to step across as the vessel rises on the swell, then sit down where you are told to and put your fins on. Fully equipped divers may wear their masks around their necks during the journey

Bigger boats have space for divers to put on their equipment when they arrive over the dive site.

so that they can defog them immediately before entering the water. The journey may be a little uncomfortable if the weather is anything more than flat calm. Some boats have the facility to allow divers to don their equipment once they arrive at the dive site.

Entering and leaving the water from a small boat

The usual method of entry is to roll backward into the water. This is either done with a number of divers entering together on a count of three or with individual divers going when they are told it is safe to do so. It is important to enter the water at the right place, but you should be careful to avoid other divers.

When you surface, you must pay attention to any instruction given to you by the crew in the boat that comes to pick you up. They may require you to swim away from the reef, where the boat would be in danger of being damaged, and out into deeper water. They will position the boat so that the prevailing wind pushes it toward you rather than away from you.

The **backward roll** is usually the preferred method for entering the water from an inflatable boat.

If a small boat is equipped with a ladder, divers will normally be required to **take off their fins** before climbing aboard.

> ### IN OVER THE TUBES
> There is a technique to getting out of the water and over the tubes of an inflatable boat. Keep your mask and fins in place and hold tightly to the beckets (rope loops) or grab line that runs round the side of the boat. Position yourself vertically in the water and then push down hard so that you are momentarily submerged. As the buoyancy of the suit sends you back up, fin strongly, and at the same time push up from the grab rail, straightening your arms as you go. You should be able to lock your arms, then lean into the boat so that your chest tilts you over. At the same time, lift one leg over the tube. You should then be able to take off your fin before lifting the other leg in and removing the second fin.

When getting into a small boat after a dive, it is common to first hand up your weights and any other loose items. After that, with your BC fully inflated so that your rig floats, climb out of your rig and pass it up. If you are familiar with your equipment, you should have no trouble doing this while holding on to the rail or grab line with one hand.

You should keep your fins and mask in place until you are safely in the boat. Some larger inflatable boats and other small dive boats have ladders, which may require you to take off your fins before climbing up out of the water.

BIG BOATS

An **expedition vessel** such as this is equipped to take divers to remote locations that are out of reach of those boats that need to return to port each night.

Day boats and live-aboard vessels

There are some advantages to diving from a larger vessel. You can go farther from the mainland, and the journey is usually very comfortable. With sufficient supplies of air and food, a larger vessel allows you to have meals on board and stay out all day. Also, dive sites beyond the range of the small boats are accessible to larger boats.

On most larger boats, there will be a lounge where you can relax in between dives and during the journey. There is also somewhere to stow all your dive gear until you need it.

You may dive from the swim platform at the back of the vessel and return to it by climbing the ladder provided. Or you may need to transfer to a smaller boat for the last part of the journey to the dive site. Sometimes, you will do a combination of the two, entering the water from the main vessel and getting picked up by a small boat later when you surface.

Some dive boats have cabins to stay in overnight. These live-aboard vessels are usually larger than day boats, but not always. They are like a home away from home and have everything you need on board. Live-aboard vessels give divers the opportunity to reach

There is usually **a swim platform** at the back of a larger dive boat equipped with a ladder for climbing back on board.

more unusual destinations.

The cabins nowadays usually have twin beds rather than bunk beds and en suite showers and toilets. The food is often very good, cooked in a properly equipped galley and eaten in a spacious lounge. Often, there are sundecks for those who want to get a tan.

Smaller boats may be used for daily diving from a land-based dive center or in conjunction with a bigger vessel.

Diving facilities
The passengers' diving equipment is usually kept at a dive deck at the stern of the vessel. There, you'll find your BC and regulator permanently mounted onto a tank and ready to go at a moment's notice. Normally, your mask and fins and other equipment are stored in a box under the seat next to your tank, while your wetsuit will be hanging on a rack.

In some areas, including the Maldives, the main vessel works in conjunction with a second large boat that keeps all the diving equipment on board.

A live-aboard dive boat will normally have its own compressor for supplying air (and many can mix and supply nitrox).

Getting around
The itineraries of diving trips are usually scheduled so that the boat travels the longer sections of the route during the night. This means that when you get up in the morning you can dive in a different location at first light.

These early morning dives are often the best of the day because it is at this time that the larger predators hunt on the reef before retiring out into deep water once the sun has fully risen.

The number of passengers on a large diving boat can vary from six to 26. If you choose to take part in such a trip, you will spend most of your time in close proximity to your fellow divers, so you need to be able to get along with them. Most groups bond fairly quickly because everyone is there for the same purpose—to go diving!

Big live-aboard vessels are like floating hotels that move to different locations between dives. The early morning dive is usually the best of the day.

DEEP DIVING

You should **never go deeper** than your certification allows unless you are on a specific training dive with an experienced instructor.

Deep diving is for very experienced divers only, but divers of all abilities should be aware of the dangerous and sometimes frightening effect that water under pressure has on their bodies.

Diving rapture

The inert nitrogen in the air that we breathe when we are under pressure has a narcotic effect known as nitrogen narcosis. Jacques Cousteau called it "the rapture of the deep."

Nitrogen narcosis affects people in many different ways. Some people become euphoric when at depth, whereas others become paranoid, and some even experience both emotions.

Not much research has been done on the subject of nitrogen narcosis. Scuba diving training agency manuals often liken the effect of nitrogen to that of alcohol—the deeper you go in the water, the more "drunk" you get.

Some people seem to be unaffected and can complete complex tasks at 160 feet (50 m), whereas other divers become incompetent at only 50 feet (15 m) deep. It is believed that the nitrogen we absorb affects the transmission of information within our nervous system.

This probably explains why experienced divers seem not to experience nitrogen narcosis, whereas new divers often do. The bodies of experienced divers have adapted to cope with the effects of nitrogen, just as hardened drinkers are apparently able to tolerate higher levels of alcohol than moderate drinkers.

Some divers start to act irresponsibly at depth, whereas others become overcautious or even fearful. In difficult conditions, such as low visibility, the effect of nitrogen narcosis appears to increase.

The dangers of nitrogen narcosis mean that you should never go to depths that you are not used to. When you are training to go deeper, you should always be escorted by someone with plenty of experience. You should never go deeper than your certification allows.

Decompression stops

At depth, you also start absorbing nitrogen quicker than you would in the shallows.

Your **diving computer** continually tracks your time and depth, and displays mandatory decompression stop information.

DECOMPRESSION STOP DIVING

More experienced divers are prepared to make decompression stops if they need to on an ascent from a dive.

When your are diving on a wreck, for instance, there is no feature to ascend except the rope to the surface. Divers make stops at different points during the ascent. If it is likely to get a little crowded on the line, sometimes a trapeze system is lowered into the water from the boat above with bars at fixed depths such as 30 feet (9 m), 20 feet (6 m), and 10 feet (3 m) from the surface. Current thinking also suggests that it is beneficial to make two-minute stops at half the maximum depth (or pressure) of the dive and half that depth again on the way up. These are known as "deep stops."

The no-stop diving times beyond 80 feet (25 m) are quite short, and it's easy to stay underwater too long. A deep dive needs to be planned carefully so that the no-stop time is adhered to. If it is not, you will have to make staged decompression stops at points during the ascent.

The first mandatory stop you will see on your computer display will be at 10 feet (3 m), but if you stay deeper longer, you may have to make stops at 20 feet (6 m), 30 feet (9 m) and even 40 feet (12 m), too.

Air doesn't last as long at depth, so you need to be sure to take enough with you to make the slow ascent required. This may mean being equipped with a larger tank or even more than one tank.

Multilevel dives

If you dive deep at the beginning of a dive and then slowly make your way back up the reef, you are doing what is called a "multilevel" dive. This gives your body enough time to shed the nitrogen that it has absorbed naturally.

Your diving computer recalculates your decompression obligation as you go. Take your time but manage your air so that you have plenty left in the shallows. A long time spent at less than 30 feet (9 m) deep makes your ascent even safer. It is important not to forget the safety stop at 15 feet (5 m).

DRIFT DIVING

The pickup boat needs to see its divers after the dive. **A flag on an extending pole** clearly marks their position.

Drift diving is what it sounds like—the diver is transported by the currents and can travel great distances beneath the waves.

In the current

Drifting on strong currents is a delight when you know that your dive boat will pick you up after you surface. You move along effortlessly, and the scenery rolls by. You can cover a lot of "ground" in a very short space of time.

It's important to stay with your buddy when you first submerge and keep together during the dive. Even in clear water, the visibility is such that you can easily be separated. Although you may be only 100 feet (30 m) apart, you'll be unable to see each other. If one diver stops for a moment, maybe finning back into the current to look at something, the other will carry on.

If you do get separated, the only thing to do is to look for any bubbles heading toward the surface. They may indicate where your buddy is. If you can't see any, make your way at a safe speed to the surface. Your buddy should have done the same. It may mean

that the dive is over at this point, depending on how long you were submerged before you became separated.

On the surface

There's not much to know about the underwater aspect of drift diving. It's what happens when you break the surface that is important. Your pickup boat needs to know where to find you.

In many circumstances, such as when you are diving in a tidal current over flat terrain, you could come to the surface almost anywhere. In this case, it is best to

The **surface marker buoy** (SMB) tells the crew of the diver's boat where he or she might surface.

DEPLOYING THE BUOY

To deploy the surface marker buoy, push the unrolled and uninflated buoy upward so that it floats above the point at which you attached it to the winder reel line. Then, hold the reel in one hand with the open end of the buoy. There are devices available that help with this. Insert your octopus rig into the open end and press the purge button firmly. The buoy will fill with air and should get plenty of air before it shoots off to the surface. Depending on how deep you are, the air will expand on the way up to fill the buoy more. Too much air will simply spill out from the bottom. The reel will become a blur as it deploys the line. Never attach a reel to yourself when you do this.

permanently deploy a surface marker buoy (SMB). To do this, you unwind the reel according to your depth, never letting out too much line in case of entanglement. The boat driver simply follows the buoy until you break the surface.

At other times, you may be following a reef or another type of topography that your boat driver is familiar with. In many parts of the world, the locals know the currents extremely well. If this is the case, it may be safe to go diving without having to use a permanent SMB.

When you decide to ascend, you can let the person in the boat know by deploying an SMB. When that breaks the surface, your boat driver will know when and where to expect you.

You should always keep your SMB inflated until you are about to get into the boat, just in case you haven't been spotted yet, even though the boat may seem to be approaching you to pick you up.

The ocean is a very big place, and you will never feel that more than when you surface and there is no boat nearby.

An SMB is not easily seen from a great distance. Where dive boats have to pick up many divers surfacing in separate groups, you will need a surface marker that is extremely easy to spot and very distinctive. A flag on an extending pole often proves effective for this purpose.

It's best to keep your SMB inflated until you make physical contact with your pickup boat.

DIVING IN CURRENTS

Two divers make their way back up the anchor line toward their boat. Divers who learn how to cope with currents get to see more interesting dive sites.

Understanding tides

The sun and moon have a gravitational pull on the Earth's oceans, causing water levels to rise and fall. The changes in water levels are the tides.

When the sun and the moon are aligned (at a full moon or a new moon), the sun and the moon pull together and the gravitational effect on the ocean is strongest. This is called a "spring" tide, when there is a big difference in the height of the low tide and the height of the high tide.

When the sun and moon are in opposition (at right angles to each other), they cancel out some of the gravitational effect. This happens during the moon's first and last quarters. At these times, there is less difference between "high" and "low" tides. These are called neap tides.

Due to the rotation of the Earth and orbit of the moon, there are two high tides a day, about 12 hours apart. The tides not only affect the depth of water over a dive site, they also affect the amount of water that floods in and ebbs out.

On those occasions when there is an exceptionally high "spring" tide, there is also an exceptionally low "spring" tide. A lot of water is shifted to and fro in the ocean in the same period of time, and the currents can be very strong. This can make diving either almost impossible or very spectacular.

Ocean currents

The land we live on stands on a continental shelf that stretches from the coasts far out beneath the oceans. When the level of the deep ocean rises with the tide, the water floods up over the shelf. When the level falls, the water ebbs back. The flow of this water is called a tidal flow or current.

Many famous diving destinations are affected by ocean currents. Out in the ocean itself, there may be only a few feet of difference in the depth of the water you dive in at different times, but the ocean currents can still be very strong. The currents are also driven by the dragging effect of winds on the ocean surface (see pages 60–61). Other causes of oceanic current are the jet stream (a band of very strong wind high above the

Current points attract the big and more spectacular predators such as this **gray reef shark**.

Earth) and changes in seawater temperatures, such as those close to the Poles.

Local currents

The seabed is not flat; it has a bumpy surface caused by natural features, reefs and even wrecks. The sideways pressure of the water as it flows onto the continental shelf means it has to squeeze around, up and over, or even through some of these obstacles. Like the air passing over the wing of a plane, the water has to speed up to get past the obstacles, causing fast currents.

In other places, vortexes, or areas of low sideways pressure, are produced. These places are said to be in the "lee" of a current.

The water squeezing up and over a reef or wreck can speed up dramatically. These areas of fast currents, or current points, often attract large marine animals.

Currents can change very quickly. You may start a dive when there is apparently little current at all, but while you are down there, the current is very likely to strengthen once again.

USING A CURRENT HOOK

A current hook is simply a length of thick cord attached to your BC by a carabiner with a big hook on the other end. To attach it, you simply choose a part of the substrate or rock that is strong enough to take it and hook it on, letting the current push you back to take up the slack. If you add a little bit of air to your BC to make yourself just positively buoyant, you will feel as if you are flying like a kite in the breeze. This is a relaxing way to float in a current and watch the big fish that are attracted to the spot on the reef known as the "current point."

WRECK DIVING

Wrecks can be fascinating places and even the most inexperienced diver will be tempted to take a look inside.

There is always something special about diving on the remains of a mighty ship that now lies on the seabed in its watery grave. Some shipwrecks got there because of errors in navigation, others were victims of war and some were sunk intentionally. Whatever the reason, there is always a story to be told.

Exploring a wreck

When you first go wreck diving, you will probably be content to swim around the outside of the wreck, marveling at the sight. It's amazing to see something that was once such a valuable object so discarded. You may venture a closer look at the twisted metal.

As you get more confident, you will want to explore further, but you need to know what you are doing.

Entering the engine room of a sunken vessel might be exciting but should not be undertaken without the right training.

Wrecks are interesting because you have access to areas you would not normally see in a functioning ship. The crew's quarters and the engine room are especially intriguing. The remains of the cargo can be fascinating, too. Although in poor condition after being immersed in seawater for so long, they remain frozen in time from the day they left the sunlight.

THE WRECK DIVER'S REEL

Wreck divers often take a small winder reel in their BC pocket or clipped to a convenient D-ring. Some training agencies insist on the simplicity of a spool. The reel should have a ratchet and lock and carry enough line for the depth. A line rarely goes up vertically—its buoy will be subject to current and wind at the surface. You will need a longer length of line than the depth from which you deploy the buoy, perhaps 50 percent extra. Never attach a reel or spool to yourself or your equipment when launching a delayed buoy or you may be dragged up with it.

Once a wreck is established, it becomes a haven for wildlife. The darker recesses harbor masses of smaller fish together with the larger ones that hunt them. These dark corners can be illuminated with the light from your lamp.

A dangerous place

Entering a wreck is not recommended without special training. It's not just a matter of taking a big dive light with you, although that is essential.

Entering confined spaces with no direct route to the surface is a serious business. The visibility may be good, but no matter how carefully you move, you will disturb the sediment on the floor. Your exhaled bubbles will knock down rust from the ceiling. You need to be careful how you move and be aware that there may be someone behind you. If the visibility was good to begin with, a single diver can make it poor in a moment. It is at that point that you realize you need to know your way out.

A diver's winder reel and line are ideal for such a situation. If you tie off your line to a convenient point outside the wreck, you can unwind it as you go in and wind it back to find your way out. You must be taught how to do this properly, because you need to belay the line—tie it off at points along your route so that it does not get pulled and take up a route you cannot later follow.

The **cargo** of a wrecked freighter can be as interesting as the wreck itself.

The **dark recesses** of a wreck act as a haven for masses of small fish.

A shipwreck is a big object, but it's easily missed if it's lying at any great depth or if the visibility in the water is not good. Your boat's captain will find the wreck by using a GPS (Global Positioning System) and an echo-sounder and mark its position with a heavy weight tied to a line and buoy. This is commonly called a "shotline." You follow the line down to the wreck, and later follow it back up to your boat.

If the wreck is very large, or there is a strong current flowing, you may not be able to make it back to the shotline, in which case you need to be able to put up your own buoy and line and ascend that.

Entering a wreck safely is not just a matter of taking a big light with you.

FRESHWATER DIVING

The water of a **freshwater lake** is often dark and turbid and the diver must take care not to stir up silt from the bottom.

Lakes and flooded quarries are favorite places for new divers to gain experience. They are unaffected by windy conditions and rarely have any currents. You can go diving in them whatever the weather. Some of them are stocked with fish, such as rainbow trout. However, large bodies of fresh water introduce other problems that a diver should be aware of.

Visibility
Some lakes may look idyllic at the surface with flat, calm water that reflects the blue sky. While lakes look very inviting, the diver often finds that the water in them is stained dark brown with peat and visibility is very poor. Most lakes have a muddy bottom and one touch with a fin, or the water thrust by a

Rainbow trout is a common species of freshwater fish.

fin, can stir it up. Even a flooded slate quarry can have high levels of detritus and algae bloom. Be aware that diving in fresh water can mean diving in the dark.

The owners of many diving sites put in suspended platforms for trainee divers to kneel on while practicing skills. These places can be very popular, especially on weekends, and a large number of divers means that visibility is more likely to be poor.

Low temperatures

One problem of diving in fresh water is the water temperature. The sea around the coasts of temperate countries rarely gets colder than 57°F (14°C), but the water in lakes can often be as cold as 37°F (3°C).

Water conducts heat away from our bodies much faster than air—in fact, about 25 times faster. This means a diver in a wetsuit fully immersed in cold water is soon in danger of hypothermia. People who dive in cold, fresh water should be properly equipped in a drysuit with suitable layers of insulation under it and wear gloves.

Regulator problems

When gas is put under pressure, it produces heat. When it is depressurized, it loses heat. The air in your tank is at a pressure probably

A regulator freeze-up causing an exponential free-flow is a real risk when diving in cold, fresh water, but a properly trained diver should have no problem.

exceeding 3,000 psi (200 bars) at the start of a dive. At the first-stage of your regulator, the pressure drops to around 116–145 psi (8–10 bars) more than the pressure around you. At 100 feet (30 m), the ambient pressure is 58 psi (4 bars). This is a huge pressure drop and, as a result, the regulator will get very cold.

Fresh water freezes at 32°F (0°C). The temperature around the first-stage can be much lower than this. Ice can cause the regulator to malfunction, making it stick open. The huge flow of depressurized air has the same effect at the second-stage, resulting in an uncontrollable free-flow of air. You will be shown how to use a free-flowing regulator, but it still means ending the dive. It's a good idea to dive with two independent regulators on two separate tank valves, either with twin cylinders or with a single cylinder that has an H-valve.

A diver should be properly prepared to face the special hazards encountered at freshwater dive sites.

UNDERWATER NATURALIST

Coral reefs teem with animal life in a vast variety of forms. Even what looks like rock has been formed by a colony of tiny animals.

One of the thrills of scuba diving is seeing marine life up close. As your diving improves, you will have more time to examine the creatures you encounter and learn more about them.

Coral reefs

It may surprise you to know that most of what you see underwater, especially in tropical areas, is animal life—even the rocks and the foliage. The rocklike parts of coral reefs are made by tiny polyps that leave a calcareous skeleton behind them as they grow. The "foliage" is actually soft coral that becomes tumescent in the current. Both types of coral feed on the minuscule plankton that pass by.

Marine fish

The marine wildlife that you are likely to see includes the little orange fish that flutter around the coral heads in the Indo-Pacific region. They are called anthias. Of the very many different species of anthias, the lyretail anthias are probably the ones you will notice

most. Feeding mainly on plankton, anthias hover in groups from about 6 feet (2 m) to 60 feet (20 m) deep. You will see mainly orange-colored females, as the purple males tend to be territorial.

Divers often encounter jacks. They are fast-swimming predatory fish that range from bar jacks and horse-eye jacks, which form schools of many thousands, to trevallies, which often hunt in small groups.

This abandoned ship's mooring buoy has been colonized by coral and territorial fish.

The largest of all the jacks is the mighty almaco, a deep-bodied amberjack with a dark olive-colored diagonal stripe that stretches from its mouth across the eye to around the dorsal fin.

The almaco jack is found in the Mediterranean, the Atlantic and the Eastern Pacific south of California. It prefers deep, open water away from reefs. Often weighing more than 110 pounds (50 kg) and more than 6 feet (2 m) in length, almaco jacks are magnificent animals.

There are various species of grouper that loiter around the reef. Some are quite small, whereas others are huge. Particularly

fascinating, they start life as males and later become females! Napoleon wrasses have an even more complicated sex life. They start life as males, later become females, and when there is a vacancy for a male, one of the females becomes a "super-male."

A pair of **spotted dolphins** makes an exhilarating encounter for any diver.

Dolphins
Every diver hopes to get close to a pod of wild dolphins. These large, air-breathing mammals live in social groups. There are many species, but the most common are the Atlantic bottlenose dolphin and the Pantropical spotted dolphin.

Special relationships
There are complex symbiotic relationships between some marine animals, such as the shrimp and the goby fish. The goby guards the shrimp's home, warning it of danger. Both animals benefit—the goby has a safe place to live and the shrimp has an alarm system. The clown or anemone fishes that live within the stinging tentacles of anemones are immune from the stings but are protected by them. Some smaller fish, including gobies, act as cleaners to larger animals, removing parasites from their skin and gills in return for a free meal with no risk of getting eaten themselves.

WOBBEGONGS
Over 6 feet (2 m) in length, the tasseled wobbegong, a type of carpet shark, lies in wait on the sea floor. Its well-camouflaged skin makes it the ultimate ambush predator. It has frilly, wormlike projections around its mouth that it uses to suck prey into razor-sharp teeth. Although not normally aggressive, wobbegongs have been implicated in many attacks upon divers, probably because they have been provoked or stepped on. A wobbegong's placid nature can be deceiving, and it is best left alone where it lies under rocky overhangs and in among the coral. The tasseled wobbegong is a wholly tropical species found in Australian waters and among the coastal reefs of the South Pacific.

This diver has an expensive **single-lens reflex camera** in a submarine housing together with an independent light source in the form of a powerful underwater flashgun.

The days when people took photos underwater that didn't come out are gone. Today, divers descend with tiny digital cameras and take success for granted.

Taking pictures underwater

The difficulties of getting good results from photography in water are often greater than taking pictures in air. It is important to reduce the amount of water through which the camera needs to look. This is because the water is usually full of particles and debris that obscure the image. To overcome this problem, you will need to get as close to your subject as possible.

You can restore the width of your picture by using the widest angle of view available on your zoom lens. Powerful telephoto zooms and electronic zooms that simply magnify an image are no use to underwater photographers.

WELCOME TO THE DIGITAL AGE

Digital photographers are obsessed with megapixels—the number of pixels, or digital points, a camera can record. This has a direct bearing on the size to which a picture can be enlarged without the pixels showing up in the image.

The file type and file-writing speeds are important if you don't want to miss the next shot while waiting for the first to record. Recording media or memory cards come in various sizes, types and speeds. The number of megabytes of information they can store denotes their size. Inexpensive digital cameras normally record in file types called jpegs. These compress the information so that it takes up less space in the memory and is quicker to write. Jpegs can be recorded in a choice of qualities.

A typical inexpensive **compact digital camera** (left) with its purpose-designed underwater housing (right).

Watertight housings

To use your camera underwater, it must be encased in a submarine casing called a housing. The most important consideration is whether an underwater housing is available for the camera you want. You should buy the two together because delay in getting the housing can mean disappointment if the item is no longer available.

The secret of **underwater photography** is to get as close to your subject as possible.

replaced by a newer version tomorrow. Most digital cameras have the ability to shoot a few seconds of video at any one time, which can be fun.

You rarely run out of space for more pictures because the number of digital pictures that can be stored on the memory card is enormous in comparison to a conventional roll of film You can also delete those that are not good while still underwater. Your memory card should be full of good pictures at the end of the dive.

If you want to know if a picture is good enough to keep, you can view it immediately after taking it using the camera's display screen or LCD.

The most reliable way to obtain good-quality color pictures is to use white light in the form of a separate flash. This can almost double the expense, but don't expect to take good, sharp, closeup pictures without an external flash unless you are in very brightly lit shallow water. Built-in flashes are of only limited use in clear water and no use at all if the water is turbid.

You can download the pictures to your computer using the software provided by your computer manufacturer or the software that comes with the camera. Alternatively, take the memory card to your local photo developer for prints.

The watertight integrity of a camera housing is dependent upon the careful maintenance of the O-rings that seal it. Some underwater housings allow the user to fit ancillary wide-angle attachments. These enable the lens to view a wider angle so you can approach even closer.

Digital cameras

Digital cameras are being developed so fast that even if you buy the latest and best available today, chances are it will be

Even inexpensive compact cameras benefit from the use of an **additional source of white light.**

CAMERA AND ACTION

Hollywood underwater cameraman **Stan Waterman**, shown here in his 80s, still enjoying making underwater videos.

Shooting video

Video cameras were miniaturized even before digital still cameras, and for this reason many divers have taken up underwater video-recording. Miniaturization has meant that submarine housings for video cameras are smaller, too, and this makes them practical for single operators to use. Video cameras for amateur use have been tiny for some time now, but the ones for professional use are now smaller, too.

Many **underwater wildlife films are** made using rebreathers and relatively small, professional format video cameras.

If you stay shallower than about 40 feet (12 m), a video camera, with its ability to color balance the electronic signal automatically, will produce very reasonable color images of the underwater world. Once you go deeper, you will need to equip yourself with some powerful lights that must be capable of emitting a diffuse and even beam.

The rules of shooting video are the same underwater as they are above the surface. You should endeavor to hold the camera still with perfect buoyancy control while your subject moves within the frame. You will need to build up shots so that you have enough material for your final video production. You will need a wide establishing shot, as well as shots of the action from the middle distance and closeup. You don't have to shoot them in that order, of course. A finished program can contain a series of events joined together into a sequence to represent something that may not have ever actually happened.

Small video cameras in **compact submarine housings** allow you to enter tight spaces, such as the confines of a wreck, to record the scene.

Video-recording tips

The same rules apply to video-recording as to still photography underwater: you should get in close to your subject. It's not necessary to get everything into one camera frame. A video camera has the advantage over a still camera of giving you the opportunity to construct a sequence from several shots later.

You should remember that although you may find one particular animal fascinating and dwell on it for a long time with your camera, your audience may get quickly bored watching the action later. A good guide is to look at television commercials that have high production values. There may well be a dozen or so different shots used in a sequence, but the whole thing only lasts an attention-grabbing 30 seconds.

When you construct your program from the footage you recorded, bear in mind that there are very few audiences that do not tire after watching an amateur underwater film

that lasts for more than 20 minutes. A good 20-minute program may have more than 250 individually recorded moments in it.

The other thing to remember if you are diving in a group is that if you find something interesting, you should not dwell on it too long. You should give other divers get a chance to take their pictures.

It is important to remember to rinse your camera housing in clean, fresh water after every dive. You should also remove and

Allow your subject to enter and leave the frame so that the **recorded moment** has a natural beginning and ending.

The latest generation of **compact camcorders** have submarine housings that fit like a glove, but still allow access to all the controls.

scrupulously clean any water-sealing O-rings, greasing them lightly before replacing them in the grooves of the housing. Humidity, which causes condensation, is a great nuisance to videographers. You should make sure that the air inside your housing is warm and dry before closing it up.

Finally, be sure that you know the difference between the operating and standby mode of your video camera. Many people have come back with very dull footage of the seabed because they thought their video camera was running when it was not, and vice versa.

DIVING IN THE DARK

At night, you may be able to spot those **smaller creatures** that normally hide away during the daytime.

Lighting up the details of the reef at night with your underwater light reveals everything in a full spectrum of vibrant color that you would never see during the day.

Nocturnal wildlife

Many creatures on the reef are nocturnal. They include predators, such as whitetip reef sharks and moray eels, that hunt at night. Crinoids, such as basketstars and featherstars, creep from their daytime hiding places to feed on the plankton. It's at this time that the coral polyps come to life, protruding out from the hard coral, waving their arms.

Strangely, many of the more easily frightened animals seem unaware of divers at night,

and they will be mesmerized by your diving light. Other creatures take advantage of this fact to make their hunting easy.

Some of the animals commonly encountered at night include rays feeding, hawksbill and green turtles browsing, goatfish probing for their supper in the sand, and crabs and lobsters parading out in the open. It's also during the night that the octopus stalks its prey of shellfish.

Some animals are considered particularly special quarries for night divers. These include the flashlight fish in the Indo-Pacific

This **marbled stingray** feeds by vacuuming small creatures from the seabed.

and the rosy-lipped batfish of the Galapagos and Cocos islands. Spanish dancers—sluglike invertebrates found everywhere in the tropics—are also wonderful to see at night.

The **octopus** hunts at night and is rarely seen out in the open during daylight hours.

Night diving

A loss of spatial awareness is the greatest challenge to the newly certified night diver. Without a visual check on where you are, you need to rely on your instruments to tell you how deep you are and in which direction you should be going. Many diving computers have their own integral lighting to help you read them in the dark.

It is essential to control your buoyancy unless you are diving over a sea floor of a fixed depth. When it's dark, it's easy to go deeper than you intend if there is no fixed visual reference and you omit to continually check your depth gauge or computer.

A reliable light is essential, and so is a backup light ready for use should it be needed. There is a huge range of lights with a variety of features to choose from, but the most important thing is to have one that functions. Backup lights are vital, as all diving lights can fail by flooding, running out of power or simply by blowing a bulb.

Always start a dive with a fully charged light and enter the water with it already working. If you don't want the light shining, block out the light rather than switch it off. This is because the lightbulb is most likely to fail during the current surge when it is switched on, and you don't want this to happen while you are underwater in the dark.

When signaling, shine your light on the signal you are making with your hand. If you wave your light so that it flashes across the field of vision of another diver, it will attract their attention.

Two different types of submersible strobe beacons.

Experienced dive guides believe that when divers are bobbing on the waves after a dive, they can only deliver one or two signals reliably. The signals they suggest using are a steady light, which means "come and pick me up when you can," and a frantically waved light, which means you have an emergency situation. A submersible strobe beacon is useful in an emergency because it emits a bright flash of light repeatedly over a very long period of time, clearly marking a position that can be seen from all angles.

The **Spanish dancer** is a colorful nudibranch that breathes through the feathery gills on its back.

HITCHING A RIDE

No diver in a movie is seen without a diver propulsion vehicle (DPV). There is a particularly memorable scene in the Bond movie *Thunderball* where a mass of divers speed through the water, each pulled by a sleek DPV. To a movie director, a diver simply wouldn't look right without one.

Why use a DPV?

Apart from cave divers, not that many divers have used a DPV. However, they are gaining in popularity. If you are loaded with multiple tanks, your dive will mainly consist of a descent and an ascent. You aren't going to be able to do a lot of swimming with such a heavy load. If that is the case, the only way to get around a deep wreck without too much effort is to be dragged around it by a DPV.

How do DPVs work?

DPVs all basically consist of a propeller driven by an electric motor, which is powered

The body of the DPV is mainly filled with large **batteries**.

A DPV can provide a lot of fun and divers can cover greater distances than they might be able to by merely swimming.

by a large battery and turned on by a switch in the handle.

Many manufacturers claim fast speeds for their DPVs, but the machines rarely live up to their promises. However, all DPVs go fast enough, and when you are using a DPV, it seems to be going a lot faster than it actually is. A diver in a sleek wetsuit, with

The diver, towed behind a DPV by a lanyard and crotch strap, steers by simply rotating the unit with one hand.

a minimum amount of equipment, will obviously offer less resistance in the water and achieve higher speeds.

Tow-behind DPVs

The most common DPVs are those where the diver is towed behind, holding onto its handles or using a tow-lanyard. Ride-on versions are very expensive. The correct technique is very important when using these powerful machines. The wash from the propeller can be very strong. If you get it wrong, the force can almost wash the hood off your head.

With a tow-behind DPV, it is very important to be above the unit's thrust so that your body does not obstruct it. The secret to getting your position right is to adjust your lanyard to exactly the right length so that you are above and behind the DPV. The lanyard is clipped to your crotch strap in such a way that it takes all the load, leaving you to merely reach out to control the DPV, operate its trigger, and steer it.

Torque is very important, too. You may not want to travel quickly, but you will want enough power to drag yourself and all your equipment through the water without effort. How you use your DPV will affect both your speed and the duration of your dive.

If you use a DPV with a tow-behind lanyard, you must be able to disconnect the rope easily. If your DPV were to flood, it could become extremely negatively buoyant. It would then be in danger of pulling you down with it.

JETBOOTS

Jetboots sound like science fiction, but they are real. The diver has a small carbon-fiber propeller unit with a brushless motor attached to each calf. Cables thread up through straps at the thighs to a control unit mounted at the waist. The propellers are powered by a battery that is strapped to the tank and substitutes for weight on the weight belt. The effect of powering off is rather like standing in a lift. You feel the initial thrust, and then you are off with no effort whatsoever. You simply bend your body at the waist to change direction. These amazing devices are made in California.

Jetboots are a "DPV" without the "V."

You should never use a DPV to ascend or descend. You must use your computer to control your ascent speed. If you use a DPV sensibly, it can be great fun.

NITROX DIVING

An advanced diver carries a second tank containing an oxygen-rich **mix of nitrox** to speed up decompression during the ascent.

Breathing air

Air is mainly made up of two gases—oxygen at 21 percent and nitrogen at 79 percent. Our bodies metabolize some of the oxygen in the air we breathe, but the nitrogen is inert.

When we put ourselves under pressure, as we do when we go underwater, our bodies absorb some of the inert nitrogen. As we go deeper and stay longer, we absorb more. The time that we spend underwater is limited by the amount of that nitrogen we absorb.

That is why divers use tables or a diving computer to calculate how long they can stay safely underwater.

What is nitrox?

Nitrox is any gas mixture composed of nitrogen and oxygen, including air. Air is known as Nitrox21 due to its 21 percent oxygen content. Most nitrox mixes used by divers are more than 21 percent oxygen and less than 79 percent nitrogen in order to reduce the problem of nitrogen absorption. Nitrox32 is 32 percent oxygen, while Nitrox36 is 36 percent oxygen.

Breathing a nitrox mix containing more than 21 percent oxygen reduces the chance of a diver getting decompression illness due

An ordinary **leisure diver** uses nitrox in exactly the same way as air but does not exceed the maximum operating depth for the percentage of oxygen used.

to staying down too long or coming up too quickly—providing no-stop times and ascent rates for air are adhered to.

You can simply adjust your decompression requirement by adjusting your computer to match the nitrox mix that you are using and, in that way, get more time underwater. There are also nitrox tables to suit different mixes.

However, oxygen has its problems, too. Pure oxygen becomes poisonous at quite low pressures. It is currently thought unsafe to breathe pure oxygen at a greater pressure than 1.6 bars underwater, and that occurs at only 20 feet (6 m) deep. Therefore, each specific nitrox mix has its own maximum operating depth, and nitrox training agencies all limit the use of oxygen to 1.4 bars of partial pressure within a mix with nitrogen.

The oxygen in air (Nitrox21) can become hazardous at 177 feet (54 m) deep. This does not affect leisure divers limited to an absolute maximum depth of 130 feet (40 m). A standard mix of Nitrox32 should not be breathed deeper than 105 feet (32 m). Some training agencies limit new divers to 100 feet (30 m). Most popular sites for diving in the world now adhere to a 100-foot (30-m) limit for leisure diving. PADI Open Water Divers with Level One training are still limited to a maximum depth of 60 feet (18 m) during training, but suitably qualified divers can use Nitrox32 to its full maximum operating depth (MOD).

An **oxygen analyzer** is used to confirm the oxygen percentage immediately prior to diving.

When using nitrox, a diver does not need any additional diving equipment, only the knowledge of how to analyze the contents of a tank before diving, using the analyzer that has been supplied by the dive center. In the future, all new divers will likely start breathing nitrox, and air for diving will only be for specialized use.

More advanced divers use nitrox to speed up their decompression stop times. They take additional tanks of rich nitrox with them on a dive and swap to use these to breathe from once they have ascended shallow enough for it to be safe to do so. The more advanced diving computers allow divers to set different levels of nitrox and to switch to the one that matches the nitrox mix the diver is breathing at any point in the dive. In that way, the computer tracks both the decompression stop time requirements and the amount of oxygen exposure accurately.

MAXIMUM OPERATING DEPTHS FOR NITROX

These are the greatest depths at which it is currently thought safe for leisure divers to use nitrox:

Nitrox21 (air)	177 feet (54 m)
Nitrox28	125 feet (38 m)
Nitrox32	105 feet (32 m)
Nitrox36	92 feet (28 m)
Nitrox50	59 feet (18 m)
Pure oxygen	20 feet (6 m)

DIVING UNDER ICE

Diving in icy water may not seem appealing, but there are a lot of reasons to try it.

Why do it?
Underneath the ice, the water is actually warmer than the air temperature, although it's still very cold. The water clarity in freezing water is remarkable. Because it's so cold, no plankton remains active, and it sinks away to the depths. This means that there is nothing to cloud the water. Underneath the ice, a ghostly light makes its way through the solid icy roof.

What you need to know
Ice divers must be protected from the cold. It is recommended that you wear a drysuit combined with the most efficient undersuit available. This can be used with an extra base layer, dry gloves and a thick warm hood. It's possible to purchase an electrically heated

You should always stay within the zone of daylight when **diving under ice**, even if it is tempting to follow marine mammals away from the entry hole.

vest, which is made from a hi-tech material and is powered by a large lithium-iron cell that is simply switched on and off.

The ice that divers are most likely to dive under is that covering a frozen lake. Beforehand, it will be necessary to cut an access hole in the ice with a suitable saw. Dropping down into the warmer water under

An **electrically heated vest** can be worn beneath the undersuit that forms the insulating layer under a drysuit.

This **roped ice diver** wears dry gloves and a mask that is integrated with the regulator.

the ice, a diver will immediately be aware that the only exit is the way in. Losing the exit hole could have dramatic consequences, so the diver must be securely roped. The rope is paid out by someone acting as a tender outside the entrance.

Frozen regulators are a serious risk (see page 107), and for that reason, the diver should always be equipped with a second and totally independent air supply.

There are regulators available today that are especially designed for use in extremely cold fresh water. Their first-stages are environmentally dry-sealed to keep the mechanism inside dry, and they are also equipped with good heat exchangers that can draw what little heat there is in the water to warm up the very cold air coming from the tank.

The second-stages are made of metal, or have large areas of metal incorporated in their construction, for the same reason. Some even have finned heat exchangers, in the form of finned metal sections, in the intermediate pressure hose between the two stages.

The scrubber unit that removes the poisonous carbon dioxide in closed-circuit rebreathers produces heat as a byproduct of the chemical reaction. This warms up the gas in the breathing loop, so many ice divers now use rebreathers.

Courses

There are special ice-diving courses available that teach planning, organization, techniques and how to avoid or solve potential problems. Selecting a site, preparing for the dive, special equipment and diver safety procedures are also covered.

Ice-diving trips to the Arctic and Antarctic are now available. You should always stay within the zone of daylight while diving under ice.

RULES FOR AVOIDING A FREEZING REGULATOR

- Use a regulator designed for use in cold water.
- Breathe gently during the dive.
- Practice breathing during an underwater free-flow by simulating one in the pool.
- Fill your tank with double-filtered air from a well-maintained compressor.
- Avoid breathing from or purging the regulator until it's fully submerged.
- Never use your octopus unless you must.
- Do not inflate an SMB or lift-bag from your octopus.
- Adhere to dive plans that use no-stop times.
- Don't dive deeper than you have to.

SEARCH AND RECOVERY

The seabed is complex, and small items dropped from the surface can be difficult to find without a systematic search.

It's amazing how something can get lost so easily underwater, especially if it has been dropped from the surface. Divers have developed some simple methods to look for lost items on the sea floor.

A difficult task

A pair of designer sunglasses, or some other valuable item, that falls overboard from a boat seems to disappear completely. This happens because even a moored boat swings in a large arc. As a result, objects do not necessarily fall through the water in a direct line to the bottom. Looking for a small item in this way is equivalent to looking for something on the ground that has fallen from an airplane. It doesn't help that even the best visibility underwater is equivalent to a fog on land.

The seabed is usually fairly cluttered. Even in harbors, there are rocks and weeds that will hide a small object, and sometimes even a big object, from view.

Going in circles

A diver may have a good idea of where to start a search, but to be sure of finding a lost object, the diver will need to look for it in a systematic way.

One simple method is to do a circular search. The diver should mark the epicenter of the intended search area with some form of stake or fixture that the loose end of a winder reel line can be attached to.

The diver should then move a suitable distance from the epicenter, unwinding a length of line on the way, and mark the point where the line reaches in some way. This mark will be the starting point of the search. Using the stake as the center of the circle, the diver swims around in a circle, searching the seabed within the circle.

When the starting mark is reached, some more line is unwound to make the radius of the search circle bigger. The diver marks the starting point again and swims around in another circle at the end of the line until reaching the starting point once more. By doing this, the radius of the search gets bigger and bigger and more ground is covered. In this systematic way, the seabed is searched in ever increasing concentric circles.

Search teams

Bigger areas can be searched using disciplined teams of divers who are spaced along a movable line. The line is used to keep their position relative to each other as they swim and search. One diver is put in charge of the search. Searching for valuable items that have been lost by third parties is really the job of professional divers.

Sometimes, divers search for things that were lost a long time ago. There used to be

The **binocular gunsight** on the wreck of the submarine USS *Apogon* in Bikini Atoll would make a treasured souvenir for an unscrupulous diver.

a tradition among diving club members of finding and recovering the brasswork from wrecks that lay forgotten. Some divers still like to do this. Items such as a ship's telegraph are regarded as the ultimate prize by some of these "wreckers" (although the one in the photograph, left, was actually bought from a store that sells material from scrapped ships).

But divers shouldn't just take what they find on the seabed. Many famous shipwreck dive sites are protected from plundering by divers. These include the wrecks of the fleet of Japanese supply ships sunk at Chuuk Lagoon (Truk) in World War II. Another is the fleet of ships sunk by the atomic bomb "Baker" at Bikini Atoll.

If you are asked to look for something underwater by a third party, to do so could put you in breach of the law. Most countries have strictly adhered-to regulations regarding any sort of underwater work.

Many divers dream of recovering **the wheelhouse telegraph** from a wreck they have visited. This one was purchased.

RAISING HEAVY OBJECTS

Knowing the weight of the object you need to lift while it is submerged is the key to knowing how big a **lifting bag** to use. This 100-quart (100-L) barrel of concrete weighs 530 pounds (240 kg) in air but displaces 100 quarts (100 L) of water, so only 330 pounds (140 kg) of lift is needed.

Lifting underwater

A quart (1 L) of water weighs about 2 pounds (1 kg). If you can displace this amount of water with 1 quart (1 L) of air underwater, you will obtain about 2 pounds (1 kg) of lift.

Any open-ended vessel can be used as a lifting device provided you can attach a line to it. It must be open ended because the air within it will expand on the way to the surface and the open end will allow this

expanding air to escape. Attach a line to the vessel so you can tie on the load.

A better solution to a lifting problem is to use a lifting bag designed for the job. These are available in a range of lifting capacities based on their volume when inflated. A good lifting bag is teardrop shaped so that it provides stable support when it reaches the surface and the wave action does not cause the air to spill from it. The best ones also have a dump valve like the one on your BC. This allows you to release air so that the lift is reduced or removed completely. It also allows you to take the bag away from the lifted object once it has been moved to a new location.

You will need to calculate the amount of lift required to move the object. This is worked out by finding the object's density and volume and then subtracting the weight of the water it displaces.

Using lifting bags

You should use a lifting bag of the right size. If you use an oversized lifting bag, the air in it will expand, causing the load to accelerate as it ascends. With a bag of the appropriate size, the excess air will spill out and the speed of the lift will remain constant.

The bag is securely attached to the load, and air from either the diver's tank or a second tank is used to fill it. A good system is to use two lifting bags. A larger one, which is insufficient to lift the object alone, is first filled. After that a smaller one is attached to the load and filled with air. The smaller one is used to control the lift and, if necessary, air can be dumped from it so that the load is carefully controlled. In this way, massive loads can be balanced so that it takes only the power of one swimmer to move them. When the object reaches the surface, it can be towed to its new location or to where a crane is available to lift it out.

The massive power provided when air displaces water can also be used to remove objects that are embedded in a muddy seabed. In this case, lifting bags will have far too much capacity to perform a lift safely. Instead, they are attached to the object at the end of long ropes so that they start their journey upward from very near the surface.

Once the bags are filled with sufficient air to wrench the object free of the mud, they move upward only a short distance before reaching the surface, and the object is left dangling. At this time, a lifting bag of a size appropriate to a properly controlled lift is attached.

A lifting bag is **teardrop-shaped** so that it does not spill air when at the surface. It's important to use one that matches the intended load.

Once a load has been made **neutrally buoyant**, you will be surprised how easy it is to move it.

WHEN THINGS GO WRONG

Getting an **injured diver** into a small boat requires ingenuity and proper techniques. These can be practiced in a controlled environment.

If you forget your computer, abort the dive—you should not try to manage the dive on someone else's equipment.

Sometimes you may need the help of another diver. If you get snagged in a loose line on a wreck, your buddy can quickly cut you free. If you have a massive equipment failure—thankfully, an increasingly rare occurrence with

When you are diving, one accident or mistake can lead to another. This is sometimes known as the incident pit. If a small thing goes wrong and is not corrected, before long a full-scale incident has developed. Always deal with any problems promptly.

Helping yourself

It is your responsibility to rescue yourself. For example, you should not continue a dive when you know you are running low on air because you know your buddy has plenty. You must finish the dive so that you do not have to resort to sharing the air of another diver.

modern gear—your buddy can provide assistance. Uncontrolled buoyant ascents feature heavily in diving incident reports. To prevent such an event, you should make sure that your weightbelt or your integrated weights are stowed correctly so that there is no danger of losing your ballast. Sensible divers anticipate problems and have the answer ready before it's needed.

Helping others

There may come a time when you encounter another diver underwater who is helpless and in danger of drowning. You should know

Diving clubs and schools run regular **rescue management courses** that can be a lot of fun, too!

what to do and not delay in doing it.

You will have been taught in training how to raise another person from the seabed. If the person in trouble is a diver, you can use the buoyancy provided by their BC, inflating it using the oral inflation valve if their tank is empty. In this way, you can make them neutrally buoyant and raise them to the surface in a controlled way. Dropping their weightbelt is a last resort: it will certainly see the body back to the surface but not in any recoverable condition.

Once at the surface, your first priority is to remove the person from danger. This means getting them out of the water. You should fully inflate their BC, orally if necessary, and call for help. If there is none nearby, you may start to give rescue breaths to the person while they are lying face-up in the water. Doing this successfully needs a lot of practice. It may be better to tow them to a nearby shore. Training agencies have differing opinions as to the priorities of a rescue, although no-one cares how you do it if it works!

You may need to administer artificial respiration and cardiac compressions. They can be very effective in reviving a casualty, but there are few recorded cases of people in warm waters surviving a drowning incident. However, cold water can help stimulate the body's reflex that closes up the airway for as long as the heart is beating, keeping the water out.

Diving clubs and schools run practical rescue courses. It is always a good idea to be trained and well practiced in life-saving and rescue skills.

THE ABC OF RESCUE

Airway
- Make sure the airway is open and unobstructed by any foreign object or the casualty's tongue.
- Pull the head back, extend the neck and clear the obstruction with a hooked finger.

Breathing
- Close the casualty's nostrils with one hand, seal your mouth over their mouth and exhale steadily into them, checking to see that their chest rises.
- Do this twice while checking for a pulse at the carotid artery in the neck.

Circulation
- Maintain the person's circulation by making chest compressions, using straightened arms and your full weight from a kneeling position.
- Compress in quick succession at a rate of around 80 to 100 compressions a minute (faster than one a second), stopping every 30 compressions to inflate the chest twice by mouth-to-mouth.
- Continue with this process until told by a medically qualified person to stop.

When **traveling to and from a dive site**, hold tight and take note of the driver's instructions.

Appreciating the job of the person driving the pickup boat will help your boat driver to work quickly and efficiently and in the safest way possible.

For most people who drive small boats, "person-overboard" drills are used very rarely. For the driver of a small boat that drops off and picks up divers, these maneuvers are a routine exercise.

Getting you there

Divers must be brought to a site safely. You will be told where to sit in the boat, and you should stay there. The weight and position of a small boat's load affects its steering and seaworthiness. The passengers should wear some form of permanent buoyancy. In the case of a diver, a wetsuit may be enough. A drysuit with the zip undone is as unsafe as

wearing a sea anchor should the wearer fall in the water. You must hold on tightly during the journey, and when you arrive at the dive site, you should wait for further instructions from your driver or guide.

Entering the water

When it is time to get into the water, the boat's engine will be in neutral or possibly turned off. At this time, the vessel is at the mercy of the waves. It is important that you follow the instructions for getting into the water precisely. You should enter immediately when you are told to do so.

Once you are in the water, you should swim away from the boat. The engine will be restarted, and the driver will need to move off. Boats are like cars with rear-wheel steering. They pivot around the front (bow) so get away from the back (stern), where the propeller is positioned, as quickly as possible.

Keeping watch

While you are underwater, the people in the pickup boat will be concerned about your whereabouts. They will stay in the immediate area, keeping watch for any diver who may surface with a problem. You should tell the boat crew the maximum time that you will be underwater or when to expect your delayed deployment surface marker buoy to emerge.

It is quite difficult to see the heads of divers on the surface in the vastness of the ocean. A visual signaling device, such as a flag or safety sausage, is essential. It is extremely hard to hear even the loudest whistle over the noise of the engine. The weather may have changed in the time you were submerged, and a storm may be about to break. These are challenging conditions for those looking for individuals floating in the sea.

Picking you up

Divers sometimes surface close to areas that can be unsafe even for small boats to maneuver. If you come up next to a reef, the boat crew may shout to you to swim out into open water. They will position the boat so that it is blown by the wind toward you rather than away from you. At this time, the wind and waves may push the boat toward the shallow part of the reef.

You must be careful how you pass your equipment up to the boat, and then climb into the vessel using the techniques you have learned. Keep your fins and mask in place until you are safely aboard. Listen to any instructions that might be given to you by the driver. Never go near a vessel that has its propeller turning. It is a good idea to save any conversations about the dive with your buddy until after everything is stowed, the boat is no longer subject to any hazard and you are safely on your way home.

If the weather has deteriorated while you were underwater, stay calm and use your **signaling device** to attract the people in the boat.

CAVERN AND CAVE DIVING

Cavern diving is often called diving with "an overhead environment."

On most ordinary dives, if things go wrong the diver can simply ascend toward the safety of the surface. That is not an option when there is a cave or cavern roof overhead.

Cavern diving

In cavern diving, the divers keep the entrance of the cavern in sight at all times. As long as they keep the window of blue daylight in view, they always know their way out to safety. Cavern diving is not for everyone. The open space of the ocean is replaced by a dark and claustrophobic world where the range of vision is only that lit up by a diving light.

Cave diving

Cave diving is a serious business because there is usually no access to the surface and no easy route out. The only way out is to follow the route back to where you came from. Without lights, the diver is in total darkness. Only those who have been specifically trained should undertake cave diving. It requires meticulous planning.

Cave divers use the rule of "thirds" when organizing their air supplies. One third of the available supply is used to enter the cave, and the second third is used to exit it. The remaining third is always kept in reserve.

The blue window of daylight reveals the way out of a cavern (left). A leisure diver surfaces inside an airspace within Chandalier Cave in the Palau islands (right) in the Pacific.

A diver explores deep inside a **Bahamas Blue Hole**. Cave diving should not be undertaken lightly.

They often carry their tanks slung on their hips. This allows them to get through narrow constrictions and to have ready access to the tank valves. Closed circuit rebreathers are popular with cave divers since they use less gas and increase their range.

THE BLUE HOLES OF THE BAHAMAS
The Blue Holes of the Bahamas are famous among cave divers throughout the world.

In prehistoric times, sea levels were lower than they are now and extensive cave systems were formed by the passage of rainwater through the soft limestone structure of the islands. Sea levels later rose and these prehistoric caves, complete with their spectacular displays of stalactites and stalagmites, were flooded. In some places, the cave ceilings collapsed and the presence of the cave systems was revealed as dark blue circular holes punctuating the lighter blue that reflects up from the shallow seabed. Some entrances to the caves are also found inland.

Leisure divers may enter **sea caverns**, but even this is not an experience suitable for everyone.

Often, a cave is prepared by building a base camp, where gas supplies and other equipment is stockpiled.

Finding the way
Caves are often labyrinths, so cave divers reel out a line to follow on the way back. Because it is absolutely dark, guidelines have to be laid. Lines have to be securely tied off at points along the route so that they keep their position. They have to be marked with direction arrows to show which way is out. It must be possible for a diver to feel these arrows in case he or she needs to find the way out in total darkness. The diver who loses the line out of the cave loses their life. It's as simple as that.

Cave divers need to take a lot of alternative lighting with them. They must be equipped with plenty of spare lighting. They usually wear helmets to help cope with the hard surfaces they may unexpectedly meet in the dark. Explorers that venture farther into caves use diver propulsion vehicles (DPVs) to pull themselves and all their equipment through the water.

Why do it?
Caves are usually filled with fresh water, and because there is no light, there are few life forms in it. This means the water has a clarity that must be seen to be believed.

Many caves contain amazing forests of stalagmites and stalactites that have been there since prehistoric times.

TECHNICAL DIVING

There are a number of disadvantages to breathing air or a single mix of nitrox underwater (see page 118). These include the dangers of nitrogen narcosis and the toxic nature of oxygen under pressure, which reduces the maximum operating depths. Technical divers go deeper than ordinary leisure divers and become liable for lengthy decompression stops on the way up. They get around these problems using simple methods, but they need to exercise careful thought.

Multiple tanks

One solution technical divers employ is to breathe from different tanks containing different gases. They do this to try to use the

Technical divers often need to make long **decompression stops**, some of several hours, on their way back up to the surface.

optimum mix for their depth. This may mean, for example, that they breathe air for the deepest part of a dive and then, once they are shallow enough, swap regulators to breathe a suitable nitrox mix to speed up their decompression. They may even swap to two different nitrox mixes—for example, they may breathe Nitrox28 as soon as they are shallower than 125 feet (38 m) and then change to Nitrox50 at 55 feet (17 m) or less.

Technical divers who do this need to plan each dive carefully. They should have a computer (and maybe a backup, too) that can change to different mixes of nitrox to match what is being breathed during the dive.

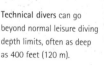

Technical divers can go beyond normal leisure diving depth limits, often as deep as 400 feet (120 m).

Oxygen toxicity

The oxygen in ordinary air may become dangerous, even fatally so, once a diver descends past 177 feet (54 m). For depths greater than that, it is necessary to reduce the amount of oxygen in the gas breathed.

Divers may need to decrease the amount of oxygen in the gas they breathe to avoid oxygen toxicity, but they also have to reduce the amount of nitrogen to avoid nitrogen narcosis.

By carrying several **different gases** in separate tanks, the technical diver can breathe the most appropriate mix of gas for the depth he is at.

Helium mixes

One way of reducing the oxygen and nitrogen content is to make up the difference with an alternative inert gas. Technical divers use helium for this. Professional divers don't use any nitrogen at all in the gas they breathe (heliox), but because helium is very expensive, amateur divers will put in a certain amount of nitrogen with the helium and oxygen. This is called trimix.

Helium brings some problems with it, too. It dissolves more readily into the diver's tissues, resulting in much greater decompression requirements. Since the diver is already going to require long stops because of the extreme depths, dive times can be in the range of several hours.

Trimix, which is suitable for use at depth, will not sustain life in the shallows. Technical divers swap to nitrox with varying levels of oxygen to speed up decompression. Some technical divers even breathe pure oxygen from 20 feet (6 m) and at the surface. This means they may dive with four tanks.

It's hard to keep warm for such a long period in the water, but helium also conducts heat away from the body faster than the other gases divers use. Often, technical divers wear drysuits that are fed with the inert gas argon or even just air.

Technical diving is a complex subject, and becoming a technical diver requires advanced training and specialized equipment.

A diver breathes **pure oxygen** at the surface to speed up the safe release of inert gases that have been absorbed during the dive.

REBREATHER DIVING

What is a rebreather?

Instead of inhaling the breathing gas and then exhaling it into the water, as a diver does with a conventional open-circuit scuba, a rebreather allows the diver's lungs to become part of a closed loop with the

A **closed-circuit rebreather** allows you to stay at depth for longer than ordinary scuba equipment, and there aren't any exhaled bubbles to disturb the marine life.

equipment. The gas is inhaled, part of the oxygen within it is metabolized, and then the gas is exhaled back into the loop. A counterlung takes up the volume of gas when the diver's own lungs are deflated.

This gas now contains carbon dioxide, which is a byproduct of breathing, and also a large amount of unused oxygen. The poisonous carbon dioxide is removed by passing it through a chemical scrubber. The oxygen level is topped up automatically before the gas goes back to the diver's lungs.

It is not the percentage of oxygen in the breathing gas but the partial pressure (ppO_2) that is crucial to its life-sustaining qualities. At deeper levels, the diver actually needs less and less oxygen for the same partial pressure.

The **PRISM Topaz** is a U.S.-made closed-circuit rebreather.

The closed-circuit rebreather (CCR) automatically maintains this at a chosen amount. The rebreather then enriches the breathing mix as the diver ascends. As a result, the amount of gas consumed is minimal. Dive times are more dependent on the duration of the scrubber material than gas supplies, so divers only need to carry small cylinders.

Advantages of rebreathers

A rebreather has two cylinders. The oxygen from one cylinder is mixed with a diluting gas (diluent), such as air or an air-helium trimix, from the other cylinder to give it sufficient volume in the loop. The built-in electronics control the mix of gases to make sure the diver is given the right mix at any time. They also track the decompression status of the diver breathing different mixes at different depths.

Because the rebreather maintains the ideal gas mix for any depth, the amount of inert gas absorbed by the diver is kept to a minimum. For example, the no-stop time for a diver using a set point of 1.3 bars ppO_2 with air as a diluent gas at 60 feet (20 m) is about three hours, as opposed to around 40 minutes with conventional scuba equipment.

This means a diver can go deeper or stay longer, or a combination of the two, than when using an open-circuit scuba, without paying the penalty of long decompression

stops. The absence of exhaled bubbles also confers a great advantage to those who want to get close to larger and more easily frightened animals. Much of the spectacular wildlife footage on television and closeup photographs of animals, such as sharks, are obtained by divers using closed-circuit rebreathers.

The author wearing an original **Inspiration CCR** unit at Cocos Island.

However, it is important to remember that the diver is now dealing with two gases, oxygen and carbon dioxide, that are potentially lethal at depth.

There are many different rebreathers available but, at the present time, only a few are in mass production, including the Inspiration and the smaller Evolution. Consequently, these are the ones most likely to be seen at dive sites. The Inspiration has been developed continuously since it first appeared. Although the basic design may look the same, the onboard electronics and computer system is now very different from the early models.

THE EVOLUTION REBREATHER

Some divers want a smaller rebreather that allows them to go deeper but not as deep as technical divers. These divers may want to be able to stay in depths at the limit of air-diving long enough to get the pictures of the wildlife they want. Also, they may want the reduced noise of a rebreather but not the lengthy decompression

stops of an open-circuit scuba. The completely new electronics and design of the Evolution rebreather fulfills these requirements. Most of its operating features are automatic, making it easy to use. The Evolution is perfect for the traveling diver who does not require the onboard gas supplies of a full-size rebreather.

CONQUERING YOUR FEARS

You can swim alongside **an underwater cliff** at your chosen depth without the fear of falling.

First fears

When you first struggle into a wetsuit and strap on that heavy tank and those big weights, it's quite disconcerting. You could be forgiven for thinking you might get into the water and sink out of sight forever!

Once you find out that doesn't happen, you have to cope with the claustrophobic feeling wearing a mask gives you. But it's even worse taking your mask off in the water. After a while, though, it becomes easy, as does taking your regulator out of your mouth and replacing it. You start to enjoy yourself, and diving becomes second nature. You can take the time to really explore the world underwater.

What should you be afraid of?

The most dangerous thing you meet when you go diving is the water around you. Claustrophobia can be a real problem for some divers, while others relish diving in places with poor visibility and restricted vision. There are plenty of places that can provide that environment, but if you don't like it, don't do it.

Once you get out into the ocean, you soon realize that it's a very big place. Agoraphobia—the fear of wide, open spaces—may envelop you. But you can overcome this as you gain confidence. The preconceptions you developed on land, subject to the laws of gravity, can now be disregarded. The water is

Poorer **visibility underwater,** often found in some
inland sites, can lead to a feeling of claustrophobia.

very deep, but that is of no consequence
because you choose the depth you swim at.
This means that you can swim alongside a
steep underwater cliff without any danger
of falling.

Another problem is overconfidence. You
may have had a fantastic first dive and go
back into the water full of euphoria. But if
the euphoria makes you overconfident, things
can go wrong. You could find yourself paying
the price for not paying enough attention to
what you're doing. If things do go wrong, it
is important not to panic as this can lead to
mistakes. You should be in control—think,
plan and act.

It is essential to develop a routine for
assembling your gear and preparing for a
dive. You can make the operation of your
equipment second nature by practicing with
it in the safe conditions of sheltered water.

You will soon discover that the sea
monsters portrayed by authors, filmmakers
and sensation-seeking journalists are only

fictional ideas that capitalize on ignorance.
Scuba diving gives you the tools to visit a
place that can otherwise only be imagined.
You will discover the reality of a world
where people can get close to the most
feared predators in the world and probably
the most misunderstood creatures on the
planet—sharks!

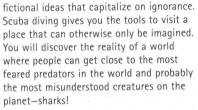

Closeup photographs like this one make sharks look
really scary. Although we may be frightened of them,
sharks are even more scared of us.

Knowledge is a powerful weapon and
diving can help you overcome preconceptions
about the underwater world. For example,
you may think that swimming in a lake full
of millions of jellyfish is incredibly dangerous.
But in Palau, an island group in the Pacific,
there are lakes that have jellyfish populations
that don't sting, and swimming among them
is an unforgettable experience.

As President Roosevelt once said, "You
have nothing to fear but fear itself."

Swimming unprotected in a lake full of **jellyfish** is fine if
you know they don't sting.

RISK MANAGEMENT

Discuss your plans with your buddy while preparing for the dive.

Managing risk

Risk management is your own responsibility. You've been told what conditions to expect; you know what equipment you have at your disposal; you know how much breathing gas you have to complete the dive; and you know how you will get back out of the water. What are the risks that you must consider?

Pressure hazards

Pressure-related problems are the most insidious because they are not visually apparent. Going deeper than you planned could mean mandatory decompression stops, which means it will take you longer to get to the surface than you anticipated. Also, your air supplies may not last as long as you expected if you go deeper than you intended. It is important to remember that your air at 100 feet (30 m) deep lasts only half as long as it does at 30 feet (10 m).

Be honest

It's your responsibility to take control. If you feel that the planned dive is beyond your capabilities, you should say so. You must never let peer pressure influence you so that you are dragged unwillingly along by the enthusiasm of the group. Bravado is misplaced on a dive deck. You must adjust the plan to suit your experience and get prior agreement from your buddy. You cannot discuss these matters deep underwater. It is vital to set limits you are happy with and stick to them.

Don't allow peer pressure to drag you into a situation you later regret.

If you think the planned dive is **beyond your capabilities**, say so. Bravado has no place on the dive deck.

Stay calm. You will be surprised how long your remaining air can last in the shallows.

What are your limits? The dive may be deeper than you are comfortable with. You may decide that, considering the size of your tank and your air consumption, you'd like to try a dive that is less ambitious. Perhaps the current is too strong for you, or you would prefer to drift with it while your buddy plans to swim against it. You may be unhappy about a plan to penetrate a wreck and would prefer to look at it from the outside only. You need to consider whether you are happy with the pickup arrangements and those for getting back on the boat. You must decide whether the surface of the sea is too rough for your liking.

Reality strikes

If you let others influence you at the planning stage, you may find that when you are underwater, things start to go wrong. Your heart rate increases, you find you are working too hard and you start to breathe quicker and quicker. There is nothing more likely to increase your air consumption than the realization that you are running low on air. Hyperventilation leads to panic.

If this happens to you, the first thing you must do is calm down. You should think carefully and act accordingly. Don't do anything in a rush—panic can have dire consequences. If your pressure gauge is in the red section, but you need to make a safety stop at 15 feet (5 m) deep, you must stay calm and breathe normally. You'll be surprised how long the remaining air in your tank will last in the shallows. Once you are at the surface, keep your mask in place and inflate your BC orally if necessary.

Next time, you'll be sure to never put yourself in this predicament. Most divers have some bad experiences, but it is important to learn from them.

Knowing your limits should ensure that you surface from every dive having enjoyed it.

HAZARDOUS MARINE LIFE

Fire coral is a common and parasitic invader of true coral. It can deliver a powerful sting to an unwary swimmer who dares to handle it.

Marine animals don't know what to make of divers. If we keep still, they will treat us as part of the scenery. If we breathe out a lot of bubbles, they will beat a hasty retreat. The bigger the animal, the more cautious it seems to be.

Plankton

Many of the lifeforms that make up plankton have stinging cells that give an uncomfortable and irritating sting. Plankton is part of the "soup" that is the basis of the food chain underwater, and it's all around you. If you want to avoid it, you should wear a full suit, of course.

In general, it is the sedentary animals that come armed with venom. Free-swimming predators can swiftly escape into the safety of the ocean's open water and don't need to use poison.

Stingers

Jellyfish are a serious hazard because some have stings that can cause anaphylactic shock. Jellyfish may be fascinating to look at as they pulsate along in their aimless manner, but if you are not sure which ones sting and which ones don't, it's best to keep away. The poisonous Portuguese man-of-war jellyfish, with its purple sail and extremely long stinging tentacles, floats around the temperate oceans of the world. The deadly sea wasp or box jellyfish is indigenous to tropical Pacific waters and kills far more people than any shark.

Fire coral, which is a pretty brown color with a white fringe, is not a true coral. It is common in shallow, well-lit water and can deliver a nasty burning sting. It has ruined many a vacation for anyone unlucky enough to come into contact with it.

Jellyfish may be interesting to watch, but do not touch them.

Venomous creatures

One animal responsible for some deaths in the waters of Queensland, Australia, is the blue-ringed octopus. It is minute and would be easy prey so it defends itself from predators with its a venomous bite.

The stonefish sits all day without moving, looking, as you would guess, like a stone. It even covers itself with weeds and algae to help with the effect. The creature uses this strategy to make itself the perfect ambush predator. As it is hardly able to move, it cannot flee predators but is armed with a set of stinging spines that makes it one of the most venomous creatures on the planet.

The scorpionfish family, which includes the stonefish, has another deadly member— the lionfish. These creatures look like wasps, and they, too, are armed and dangerous. Another animal to avoid is the pretty cone shell. This marine snail can shoot out poisonous darts.

All these animals are often encountered, so dive with your eyes and not your hands. Never touch anything unnecessarily.

Beware of sharks and stingrays

Sharks have a very effective set of teeth so don't annoy them. If you leave them alone, they won't bother you. Sharks are timid and usually stay well clear of divers.

Stingrays are not normally considered hazardous to divers, but they can harm you if they are aggravated.

The **stonefish** is one of the most venomous creatures found in the ocean. It looks remarkably like a stone covered in weeds.

The venomous **scorpionfish** is difficult to see unless it moves or you shine a light on it.

The **lionfish** has markings that make it look a bit like a giant wasp.

TREATING STINGS

To treat a sting, first remove the injured person from the water. The toxins of the more powerful stinging animals can be broken down by intense heat. This can be applied by immersing the area of the body affected as soon as possible in hot water. It should be as hot as the person can bear and should be applied for as long as the pain persists. Always seek medical help immediately.

Jellyfish, fire coral and anemone stings can be treated by removing any tentacles stuck in the skin and applying vinegar. Never allow fresh water to come into contact with the skin as this will cause any remaining stinging cells to activate.

CONSERVING THE PLANET

Scuba divers see things that others limited to the view from land do not. Sometimes, the view is a little worrying.

Many of the coral reefs of the Indian Ocean were destroyed almost overnight when the symbiotic algae died. This was due to a sudden rise in sea temperature. Some are slowly recovering.

Ecological disaster
In 1998, the Indian Ocean experienced a slight rise in temperature. It affected the algae that lives in association with coral and gives it its color. The coral bleached in a swathe from the shores of Kenya in the west to the islands of Palau in the east. The islands of the Maldives, famous for massive banks of endless coral, were badly affected. The coral later died and turned to rubble.

On the Malaysian island of Sipadan, its once healthy colony of turtles was left to browse among the rubble of the coral that had been smashed to pieces by waves.

In the Seychelles, what was once vibrant coral growing on a granite substrate became weed-covered corpses of their former selves. Many of the individual reefs that make up Queensland's Great Barrier Reef became covered in parasitic algae and died.

It was only scuba divers who witnessed this dramatic change. Although the coral is making a slow recovery in some parts, it gives us an insight into how fragile the ecology of our planet really is. It is a dire warning for the future and how humans can affect the environment.

A hawksbill turtle searches for food among the coral rubble of a dead reef.

Pollution
Untreated sewage pumped out from our shores kills life underwater. Pollution by phosphates from agriculture in fields runs off into rivers and the sea. This causes an imbalance

Dead coral invaded by green weeds off the outer islands of the Seychelles.

SHARK FINNING
More than 100 million sharks are caught each year for the Chinese sharkfin soup market. As the Chinese economy booms, the price of sharkfin soup also increases. With a population of 1.3 billion, demand in China is unstoppable. Poorer countries are sorely tempted to give shark-fishing licenses to the Chinese in return for financial aid, but this offers only a short-term advantage. Sharks are responsible for the health of the other animals in the sea. They eat the ill and dying so that there is no risk of an epidemic of disease. Without sharks the local fish populations die out and with them, the local fishing. Without sharks, the health of all our oceans is put at risk.

in the level of lower lifeforms. Many oceanographers believe that industry and modern farming is responsible for overdosing the oceans with nitrogen, carbon, iron and phosphorous compounds. The Mediterranean and the Sea of Japan are both now seeing plagues of jellyfish every summer because their population growth has been stimulated by the unusual levels of chemicals. At the same time, the higher predators are dying at an alarming rate.

Overfishing
There is no form of industrial fishing used today that is ecologically viable. Swordfish and bluefin tuna in temperate seas are being overfished to the edge of extinction. Turtles are caught in nets and also die in their thousands after choking on plastic bags that they mistake for jellyfish. Other animals that are caught but have no market value are simply dumped, dead or dying, back into the sea. Large populations of fish that were a valuable resource have dwindled so that they are no longer viable.

Those of us who venture underwater witness what is happening, and it is up to us to tell those who only see the ocean as a place to dump unwanted garbage.

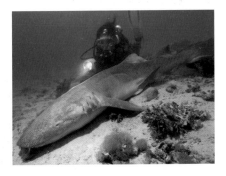

A diver examines the corpse of a nurse shark, killed for its liver and dumped back into the sea.

143

CAREERS IN DIVING

Taking care of a newcomer to scuba diving can be a very rewarding experience.

When you develop a passion for something, you want to immerse yourself in it. This is literally true for those who enjoy scuba diving! What better way to spend your life than doing something you love?

Diving instructors

As with most occupations that people easily fall in love with, there is a competitive element that affects its value in monetary terms. Like ski instructors, scuba instructors do it for the lifestyle that comes with it rather than the money they earn. In fact, it may surprise you to know that your diving instructor earns very little, if anything at all.

Someone who wants to teach diving professionally must be totally dedicated to following all the steps and climbing the ladder to become an open-water instructor. The problem is that once divers are newly qualified, many decide to go on to further levels of certification by doing more courses.

This often leads to a desire to be an instructor. So scuba instructors end up teaching newcomers who may one day compete with them for their own jobs. Many instructors go on to certify as instructor course directors so that they can earn money teaching more people to be instructors...and so on.

Working as an instructor gives you the chance to live and work somewhere exotic. Such a lifestyle is desirable, but to achieve it you will inevitably need other skills, too. Diving instructors are sought after if they

Ancillary skills, such as knowing how to handle and maintain a boat, can be just as important as the ability to teach diving.

144

Teaching diving is more about lifestyle than income. It often gives people the chance to live somewhere exotic.

also have knowledge of building construction, carpentry, electrical installations, boat engine mechanics and underwater photography—although, thanks to the advent of digital photography, this is no longer seen as scarce. In poorly supplied remote locations, diving instructors need to be resourceful people.

Other diving professions

The demand for professional divers to work in the oil industry has diminished with the advent of more cost-efficient remotely operated vehicles (ROVs) that never need to rest—nor do they suffer the medical problems associated with saturation diving. In any case, oil industry jobs are more about welding and cleaning than diving.

Some people qualify with degrees in marine biology, but there are few diving jobs that demand their skills—except, maybe, working on a fish farm.

Teaching others to dive can be a rewarding experience. By teaching someone to use scuba equipment safely, you are giving

them the opportunity to visit a new and undiscovered world. It is especially rewarding if that person overcomes some psychological difficulties on the way, such as claustrophobia. If you like working with people, you'll enjoy seeing them progress from those first nervous steps in the shallow end of the pool to being out in the ocean and meeting animals and exploring shipwrecks. Being a diving instructor is a job particularly suitable for young people

Being a scuba instructor is a **fulfilling job**, ideal for those who enjoy meeting people and are good at communicating information.

taking a break from full-time education or for older people who can afford to pursue their passion.

If you want to train to be a diving instructor, whether a volunteer in a club environment or a professional with a school, you must continue to build on your diving skills after becoming a certified diver and take all the necessary courses.

Enjoying **working with people** is a prerequisite for teaching scuba diving.

UNDERWATER ARCHAEOLOGY

An **ancient anchor** embedded in the sand can give a clue to the whereabouts of an historic shipwreck.

Amateur help

Archaeologists are thought of as the keepers of our national heritage. However, amateur divers have also made a major contribution to nautical archaeology. A number of amateur divers have found archaeological sites of great importance.

An ancient ship's anchor embedded in the sand may denote the presence of the remains of a wreck. Once an archaeological site of importance has been identified, amateur divers often work on the site, survey it and bring up the remains.

Major sites

Since prehistoric times, the sea levels have risen. Early settlements were often made at the water's edge. As the sea level rose, they became submerged and preserved under a layer of silt. A good example of this can be found along the coast of Israel, an area that had many Neolithic settlements.

When the Aswan Dam was built across the Nile River in Egypt, the annual volume of

---

THE *MARY ROSE*

The search for and discovery of the wreck of the *Mary Rose* was the result of the dedication of one man, Alexander McKee. In 1965, in conjunction with the Southsea branch of the British Sub-Aqua Club, he initiated the project to find the ship's remains. The *Mary Rose* is the only 16th-century warship currently on display anywhere in the world. It is housed at the

Royal Naval base in Portsmouth, England. The ship was one of the first ships designed to fire broadside (from cannons on one side of the ship). It sank accidentally while sailing out to engage the French fleet in 1545. The rediscovery of the *Mary Rose* and the recovery of its parts were a seminal event in the history of nautical archaeology.

An archaeologist surveys a **Neolithic village hearth**. It was revealed after its covering of silt was shifted by a storm.

Ancient bronze **soldiers' helmets** recovered from the sea.

silt being deposited into the Mediterranean declined. Now, each time the sea is rough, the silt that is already there gets moved, revealing all sorts of historical evidence. The Israeli Antiquities Authority employs a team of divers whose job it is to survey likely areas after storms, looking for signs of Neolithic settlements.

Because the Israeli coast is without any natural harbors, the remains of ancient shipwrecks—Roman, Greek, Phoenician, Persian and Ottoman—are often uncovered, together with the metal artifacts that belonged to those who were on board.

The window of opportunity for retrieval of these important pieces of history is a small one. As soon as they are uncovered, they begin to deteriorate. The Antiquities

Authority uses the enthusiasm of amateur divers in pursuit of its important work.

Another fascinating site is that of HMS *Endymion* in the Turks and Caicos Islands. This British warship carried 44 guns on two decks and had nearly 300 men aboard. In August 1790, about 18 miles (30 km) south of Salt Cay, the ship struck rocks. Today, the anchors and chain; piles of hardware that broke through as the vessel tilted; and iron ballast, bronze pins, lead hull-sheathing, tacks, musket and pistol shot, cannonballs and cannons all lie scattered where the ship's bow struck.

Nautical archaeology is a painstaking and thorough procedure that is very weather dependent. Many government agencies, museums, universities and private consulting firms employ the services of volunteer divers to work alongside underwater archaeologists. If you have a love of history and are competent working underwater, it is worth investigating whether divers are needed. Amateur archaeology is certainly a rewarding and enjoyable pastime.

Archaeology is not always ancient. A diver explores the World War II wreck of the *Scire*, a famous Italian submarine.

147

HEALTH AND NUTRITION

Fresh foods, and vitamin supplements if needed, are part of a **healthy lifestyle**.

Diving health

Brainpower is more important than brawn when you are diving. Good divers use their brain and equipment rather than their muscles to maneuver underwater. They control their buoyancy and expend as little energy as possible during a dive. In that way, they can keep their heart rate and their air consumption low.

Diving is not a competitive sport. It is an activity suitable for adults of all ages. Many of the pioneers of scuba diving, now in their 80s, are still diving regularly.

Lost fitness

When we are young, we are usually fit and healthy. Children are often on the go from

the moment they wake until the moment they finally fall asleep. We normally carry this fitness with us into young adulthood. After that, we may adopt a sedentary lifestyle, spending many hours behind a desk each day. This is combined with a diet that is based on convenience rather than good nutrition. When you add to this the fact

Children are normally fit and healthy because they are constantly active.

British Olympic cycling gold medalist and keen diver **Chris Boardman**. Not every diver needs to be as fit as Chris, but cycling instead of driving everywhere can help you stay in shape.

Reduce the amount of alcohol you drink. Apart from being full of calories, drinking too much can weaken your resolve to eat well, making that high-calorie takeout meal much more appealing. It is also important to walk or ride a bicycle instead of driving.

Today, raised levels of blood pressure are common. You can combat this by reducing your salt intake. Salt is added to nearly all processed foods, so cut them out of your diet. Eat fresh foods instead. Losing excess weight can also reduce your blood pressure.

Cholesterol can collect on artery walls and reduce the blood's ability to flow, increasing your blood pressure and making decompression illness more likely. Losing excess weight and eating wisely helps control cholesterol. This includes eating plenty of fiber and the supernutrients found in garlic. You should reduce the amount of saturated fat, such as that found in butter, in your diet and add oily fish, such as salmon, mackerel and sardines, to improve blood circulation.

that we have little time to walk or ride a bicycle, and instead travel everywhere by car, it is no wonder there are more obese people in the world than ever.

A healthy lifestyle

Good health for diving is more to do with healthy living than any special exercise regime. Breathing cold air from a regulator can use up a lot of body heat, and this is where most of the calories are burned. Divers only need physical strength for walking down to the shore or climbing the ladder of the boat.

Good health starts with your diet. Instead of sweets and salty snacks, you should eat fresh or dried fruit and nuts. Instead of sweetened carbonated drinks, drink plain water. Replace all refined carbohydrates, such as white bread and rice, with whole-grain versions. Try having oatmeal for breakfast instead of processed cereals. Pasta, tortillas and sweet potatoes are better for you than french fries. Stick with lean meats, fish, chicken, legumes and beans for your supply of protein.

Champion free diver **Umberto Pelizzari** uses yoga as part of his fitness regime.

FIT TO DIVE?

attacks when diving as a result of putting the body under stress. This stress may be triggered if things go wrong underwater or just by the difficulty of struggling down to the water's edge with heavy gear. Surface swims or even climbing the ladder of a boat in rough waters also puts strain on the body.

People who are overweight are often passed as fit to dive, but equally often they have medical conditions associated with their physique that mean they cannot dive.

Problem conditions

In the past, people who suffered from asthma were always simply banned from diving, but now medical science differentiates between different forms of the illness. If you are asthmatic, you should check with your doctor about whether you can dive.

Diabetics are disqualified from diving by many of the training agencies but not all. If you are likely to suffer a hypoglycemic attack, underwater is no place to be. Again, there are different types of diabetes, but if you suffer from it, you should check with your doctor before taking up diving.

Anyone with any form of lung disease or circulatory problem should avoid diving. If you suffer chronic back pain or have recently

Free divers, who dive without scuba equipment, obviously need to be really fit to cope with the extremes of their sport, but how fit do you need to be to scuba dive?

Diving stresses

It would seem, judging by the variety of people who go diving, that you don't need to be fit at all. However, people do suffer heart

Jumping in is easy enough, but this diver may not be fit enough to climb back aboard the boat later.

150

If you use an **inhaler for asthma**, consult a doctor before you take up scuba training.

diving. You should check with your doctor if you are concerned about this or any other medical condition.

If you are using any prescribed medication, ask your doctor about any contraindications that might preclude diving.

suffered a back injury, you should be extremely careful when strapping on heavy diving gear.

A fairly large proportion of the population (about 20 percent) unknowingly has a patent foramen ovale (PFO), also known as a hole in the heart. This genetic condition is suspected as a factor in some cases of decompression illness. However, it can be hazardous to test for and does not necessarily preclude a person from scuba

Pregnancy
It is recommended that women should not dive when pregnant, but there are many cases of such advice being inadvertently ignored. This is because many women divers were unaware that they were in the early stages of pregnancy when they went diving. There has never been any research done on the effects of diving on pregnancy, and no one is prepared to say that it's safe. If you know you are pregnant, it's best to avoid diving.

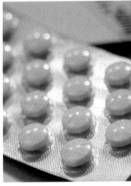

Medical checks
Few doctors are fully aware of the implications of breathing compressed air underwater. As a result, they often err on the side of safety

Some prescribed medicines are not compatible with diving.

and may preclude someone from the activity who would otherwise be fit and safe to dive. There are medical referees listed by most of the training agencies, and it is best to visit your doctor with a list of these contacts or ask to be referred to one for a full diving medical examination.

> **THE BODY MASS INDEX EXPLAINED**
> The body mass index, or BMI, is a measurement of obesity. BMI uses a mathematical formula that takes into account a person's height and weight in order to work out how much fat they have on their body. The BMI is usually calculated by dividing a person's weight in kilograms by their height in meters squared (weight ÷ height x height). It can also be calculated by dividing their weight in pounds by their height in inches squared and multiplying by 703. If the figure calculated is greater than 24.9, the person is overweight. If it is greater than 30, the person is clinically obese. It is not a totally reliable guide. As muscle tissue is heavier than fat, some athletes have a high BMI.

FEELING UNWELL?

If you have trouble **clearing your ears** during a descent, go up a little and try again.

If you become ill just before setting off on an expensive diving trip or while you are away, it can ruin your vacation. However, there are things you can do to help yourself.

Coping with a cold

You can't stop people coughing their cold germs on you, especially in the confined space of an airplane. If you think you've got a cold coming on, you need to do something about it as an infection can stop you from clearing your ears.

Prevention is better than a cure. You can boost your immune system and prevent colds by eating plenty of foods that are rich in vitamin C, such as most fruit and vegetables, and consuming friendly bacteria, such as those in live yogurt. Garlic contains super-nutrients that block the action of the enzymes that allow viruses and bacteria to invade the respiratory tracts and lungs.

If you get a cold and your sinuses are blocked up, take a decongestant pill an hour

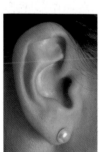

Congestion from a cold infection may cause **ear problems** for divers.

Sugar-free **chewing gum** can help keep ears free of infection.

This **special mask** stops the ears getting wet. The ear pockets are part of the same sealed pocket of air that keeps the eyes dry.

before diving but make sure that it is a type that has been tested for use under pressure.

Ear problems

You may be surprised to learn that some types of chewing gum can help stop ear infections. Sugar-free gum that contains the sweetener xylitol has been proven not only to reduce the chances of tooth decay but also to prevent ear infections. Scandinavian research has shown that xylitol can migrate into the Eustachian tubes to provide a nonstick surface that prevents the bacteria from taking hold.

If you regularly suffer from ear infections, there is a mask available that stops seawater coming into contact with your ears. It has ear pockets connected by tubes to the main air pocket of the mask and is very effective.

A drop of **olive oil** in the ear helps to prevent ear infections.

Too much sun

Sunburn can ruin a diving trip. You should try to stay out of the sun between dives. In the tropics, harmful ultraviolet rays will penetrate even if it is cloudy. Out at sea, the breeze will keep you cool, and you may not notice that you are burning. It is best to stay in the shade. In Australia, the motto is: "Slip, slap, slop!"—slip on a shirt, slap on a hat and slop on some sunblock.

Seasickness and stomach problems

Seasickness sufferers should avoid boats that go to sea for long periods, but there are medical remedies available that can be used by divers to ease seasickness symptoms. Seasickness is caused by your senses receiving conflicting signals—your ears say you are moving when your eyes say you are not—so you should avoid sitting below deck. Everybody is susceptible to seasickness at some time. Those that seem to be fine are often busy doing many things and not focused on one detail.

Upset stomachs are common with travelers in the tropics. You should drink only bottled water or drinks that have been sealed. It is best to avoid ice, unwashed fruit, salad and ice cream. If affected, you can use oral rehydration salts to prevent dehydration.

Don't dive if you don't feel up to it.

THE BENDS

Always **ascend slowly** from every dive.

Scuba diving is a relatively new sport and, in its early days, had a reputation for being dangerous. Today, the statistics show that scuba diving is not that dangerous. It does not even feature in the list of the 10 sports most likely to lead to a fatality (which does include horseback riding and fishing!). Millions of dives are made around the world every year without incident.

The bends
The main danger of diving is decompression illness (DCI), or "the bends." This is a serious hazard. At worst, it can be life threatening.

To avoid decompression illness, you should always ascend slowly from every dive and make a safety stop between 16 feet (5 m) and 10 feet

(3 m) from the surface. You should dive well within the parameters allowed by your computer and make decompression stops when and where required. It is sensible to leave long intervals between dives.

In the event of someone making an unusually fast ascent, missing mandatory decompression stops or feeling unwell in any way after diving, it is best to assume the onset of decompression illness and take measures to reduce its severity.

Treating the bends
Administering pure oxygen is an effective treatment for decompression illness. By breathing nothing but pure

Thankfully, leisure divers rarely suffer from **decompression illness**.

oxygen, the pressure gradient for the nitrogen that is still in solution within the tissues is increased. At the same time, no nitrogen is inhaled. Many technical divers breathe pure oxygen as a routine measure after a dive with a particularly aggressive decompression schedule.

All dive boats should carry an **emergency oxygen therapy set,** shown here, and an extra cylinder filled with sufficient oxygen.

Most scuba instructors are certified for the administration of pure oxygen as an emergency therapy measure in cases of suspected decompression illness. All properly equipped vessels used for scuba diving will carry an emergency oxygen therapy kit.

The rule is to give plenty of oxygen and to give it as soon as possible. The limited supplies of oxygen available usually mean that oxygen poisoning is not possible, although short air breaks can be given every 20 minutes. The casualty should be made comfortable and reassured often. The oxygen is given via a demand valve if the person is conscious or via a constant flow mask and artificial ventilation procedures if not. It is sensible to assume that the casualty's buddy is also likely to be suffering from decompression illness even if there are no obvious symptoms.

The proper, long-term treatment for decompression illness is a medically managed program of recompression in a hyperbaric chamber.

AVOIDING DECOMPRESSION ILLNESS

Even if you follow the ascent rate suggested by your computer, there is still a period immediately after you surface when nitrogen is still dispersing. This period is the "surface interval"—the time between dives. This should be as long as possible, to avoid reentering the water with residual levels of nitrogen still absorbed in the body. If you do a two-tank dive, one shortly after the other, be sure to keep to no-stop diving times and wait at least an hour between dives. Using nitrox in combination with a computer set for air can add an extra level of caution.

Some cases of DCI have been associated with dehydration as a result of alcohol consumption. It has also been suggested that hot baths or showers after diving could bring on DCI. It's probably a good idea to avoid alcohol before a dive or having a hot shower immediately afterward.

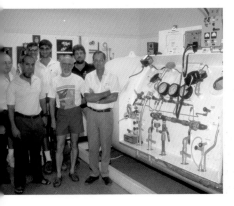

A recompression chamber in a hyperbaric facility with some of the staff who operate it.

PLANNING A TRIP

Choose a location that has the type of diving that interests you, such as **reef diving**.

There are many factors that need to be considered when planning a diving trip. These include who is going, how much time you have and how far you are prepared to travel. You also need to think about your underwater interests, the other activities that might be available, what time of year you are going and how much you can afford to spend.

What type of holiday?

If you have only a weekend to spare, you'll need to dive somewhere close to home. If you have a month to spend diving, you can go much farther away. If it's a family vacation, you'll have to think of the activities that non-divers can do while you're diving. If you have children, it will need to be at a location suitable for their needs, especially if your children want to try diving.

If you are traveling alone or with a diving partner, a holiday on a live-aboard vessel will allow you to dive all day and sometimes at night. But, if you have a non-diving spouse, this is probably not a good idea.

Some destinations look idyllic in the brochures but involve a long, complicated journey, sometimes with parts of the trip in a small airplane. Other destinations allow you to shore dive directly off the beach. This often has the benefit that you are away from

Shore diving can involve long and arduous walks with **heavy equipment**.

WHERE TO GO DIVING

Remote locations always look idyllic, but they can be difficult to get to and may require a flight in a light airplane.

If you want your **children to dive**, check first to see if both conditions and local laws allow it.

your family for hardly more than an hour at one time. On the other hand, shore diving can involve strenuous walks across hot beaches while carrying heavy equipment. A number of locations provide boat diving, although a beach launch may not suit those that are less than robust.

It's not considered safe to fly within 24 hours of doing a leisure dive. This is because airliners operate with cabin air pressures lower than that of sea level. If you have only a week to spare, you'll have to bear this in mind. You may only get five days of diving on an eight-day trip. That may be plenty if you're on a live-aboard vessel because diving is almost all you'll be doing.

Other considerations

If your interest is mainly wreck diving, you may get bored looking at reef life on every dive. If you're main interest is marine life, you may find being stuck with wreck divers is not to your liking.

You should also check what time of year is best at your destination. Everywhere has

definite seasons. Avoid going to the tropics in the rainy season, unless you do not mind torrential rain while you are on vacation.

The cost is obviously a major factor. You may be dreaming of a trip to Bikini Atoll, but may only have the budget for somewhere closer to home. You will discover that there is good diving to be had everywhere. If you do some research first, you will know what to expect.

Finding information

It is useful to look at articles in diving magazines and especially at the advertisements for specialized diving travel operators. You can then go to their web sites for more information. The bigger, independent diving web sites, such as divernet.com, contain lots of ideas and information. Best of all, speak to friends who have already been to a destination and ask their advice.

Basing your diving at a **busy resort** may ensure that those who are left behind do not get bored.

157

MARITIME LAWS AND REGULATIONS

Know the law

Divers must obey the law in the countries where they dive. Some countries have very strict and specific laws regarding the use of underwater breathing apparatus, while others have none. It's important to know what the laws are and to abide by them. It is always a mistake to assume that the laws of your own country apply when diving elsewhere. If in doubt, ask the local dive center.

For example, the United Kingdom has specific rules about diving around wrecks that have been designated as war graves. Diving on or near protected and historic wreck sites is banned altogether. Any material that is raised from underwater must be reported to the Receiver of Wreck. The U.K. law also states that professional diving instructors must be equipped with a second completely independent air source and must be under the supervision of a responsible person at the surface who acts as a diving supervisor.

Knowing the **local laws and regulations** will ensure that diving activities are not interrupted by the authorities.

Many countries have areas designated as marine reserves. Divers that visit these areas must fulfil the local requirements regarding the notification of their intentions. They must supply identification by lodging personal details with the local authority that administers the marine reserve.

Some European countries have very specific laws regarding the certification level of divers and the dives they can do. Recompression chambers or private medical insurance may be compulsory.

Dive boats are required to fly the international "A" flag while divers are in the water but not during journeys to the dive site.

Egypt not only has rules about who is certified to dive in its national marine parks, but it also specifies a minimum schedule of safety equipment that every diver must be equipped with. This includes a diving light, a visual surface signaling device, such as a flag or safety sausage, and a whistle. The maximum depths to which people are allowed to dive are specified.

Many countries issue a permit to dive, which is, in effect, a direct tax. In other countries, it is normal to pay a custom fee to the local chief of the village that owns the reef you wish to dive on. In the Maldives, a very popular diving area, there is a sweeping 100-foot (30-m) maximum depth limit to diving, and fish feeding is banned. In Florida, feeding fish, except for the purposes of harvesting (fishing), is also against the law.

Boat law

Every country has laws and regulations regarding the use of boats. They can be as simple as a limit on the number of people a vessel is licenced to carry. Others are more complicated, such as getting permission to leave port that includes a declaration of the number and identities of those on board and the intended destination of the vessel.

The **international "A" flag** is a blue-and-white pennant.

Leisure divers on vacation usually assume all the paperwork is in order and no laws are being broken.

In territorial waters, a vessel will fly the flag of the country in which it is registered at its stern and a courtesy flag of the country it is visiting at its masthead.

In Europe and in most parts of the world, a vessel that is escorting divers is required to fly a pennant known as the alpha flag, or "A" flag, while the divers are actually in the water. This is a white pennant with a blue rear half and is of a specified size and displayed at a particular height. It tells other vessels to keep clear.

This U.S. dive boat has the **red flag with the diagonal stripe** permanently painted on its side.

In U.S.-administered territories, a red flag with a white diagonal strip is the flag used to indicate that there are divers down in the water. To avoid confusion, some boats will fly both flags.

Local law rules

Local operators will always know the local laws and want to operate within them. You should be guided by them and never flout the law because it does not agree with the law in your own country. You should be aware that most countries have a minimum age limit for scuba diving.

TEMPERATE WATERS

Temperate waters can provide excellent diving, but because the water is cold for most of the year, it's best to use a drysuit. Wrapped up well to avoid getting cold, divers can often enjoy excellent short-range visibility even if the water is green.

Tidal diving

The seas around a lot of coasts are subject to tidal ranges that can be quite marked in the difference between high and low water. This means that dives have to be planned using local tide tables. Divers enter the water and conduct the dive at the optimum time, usually in the interval between the changing tides. This is called the "slack" water. Careful planning is very important. Often, it is necessary to wait a while until the time is right for a successful dive. This time is used to discuss the dive and to make sure that

Visibility may be reduced in temperate waters, but contrary to myth, there is little danger of divers becoming entangled in kelp.

everyone understands and will stick to the agreed dive plan.

Slack water only lasts 20 minutes or less, and because the water is usually still moving slightly, divers can easily get separated in the first moments of a dive. There are only three periods of slack water in any 24 hours, and some of these can be at night. It is important that the dive is not interrupted by

It is important not to miss the small window of opportunity that comes with slack water by not having your gear rigged and operating correctly.

A diver inspects a mussel rope in a Scottish lake.

Camaraderie is an enjoyable part of expedition diving in remote locations.

incorrectly rigged gear or some other problem, so performing buddy checks immediately before entering the water is essential.

Visibility

Long-range visibility can be very limited at depth, and it can be variable. Plankton blooms in summer can reduce the range of visibility to less than 3 feet (1 m) at times. A reliable diving light is an essential piece of equipment that allows each diver to know where the other is.

It is impossible for people in the boat to know where the divers are, so unless the dive is around a fixed position, such as that provided by a buoyed wreck, one diver of a buddy pair takes a surface marker buoy. It is deployed on its line from a reel according to

the depth of water. The buddy makes sure to stay with the diver holding the reel. In that way, the divers may cover a large area of the seabed during a dive, drifting along effortlessly with the current.

Where to dive

Good temperate water diving is found in many places. Around the coast of the United Kingdom, the western reaches of the English Channel, littered with war wrecks and accessed from Devon and Cornwall, the coast of Wales, and the Western Isles of Scotland offer great diving. Other famous areas that offer excellent temperate water diving are Norway, the coast of Vancouver Island, Canada, including the Inner Passage, and the Poor Knights marine reserve in New Zealand.

Because diving in temperate conditions is less popular than in the warm waters of the tropics, divers need to be more self-sufficient. They can often find themselves diving where there are no other divers. Diving in locations where there are no formal dive centers can mean that dive trips take on the format of an expedition. This appeals to ready-made groups of divers, such as dive clubs, and the friendship and camaraderie that develop between the participants give these expeditions a special character.

Summertime in temperate seas can make for a wonderful experience.

THE CARIBBEAN

White sand, a turquoise sea and shady casuarina trees epitomize the **Caribbean experience** during the main part of the year.

The Caribbean is the first-choice foreign destination for divers from the United States and Canada. The area is subtropical and stretches from the north coast of South America to the Gulf of Mexico. It is enclosed by the Leeward and Windward Islands on its eastern side. The south coast of Cuba is the northern boundary of the Caribbean Sea, but for the purposes of diving, the islands of the Turks and Caicos, the Bahamas, which are dotted across the Atlantic from Cuba to Florida, and the Florida Keys are included in the Caribbean.

When to visit

The best time to go is during the first half of the year, when the weather is settled, although there can be rain at any time. During the late summer and early autumn, big storms can develop, even becoming hurricanes. Most of the islands of the Caribbean have white, sandy beaches. There are some exceptions, including the volcanic island of St. Lucia with its black sand.

Places to dive

Destinations famous for diving include: the sponge-clad walls of Bonaire in the Netherlands Antilles, the fast drift dives of Cancun in Mexico, the steep walls of the Cayman Islands, the spectacular wreck of the Italian cruise liner the *Bianca C* in Grenada, the untouched marine park of Grand Turk in the Turks and Caicos Islands, and the shark-populated reefs of the Bahamas.

Every island in the Caribbean area that is surrounded by deep water can provide high-quality diving that is often relatively unchallenging. Visibility tends to be very good all year round.

Caribbean creatures

The soft corals of the Caribbean are of the less colorful type, but there are always

The **steep reef walls** abutting deep water are festooned with tube sponges.

Some of the creatures found on the reefs of the Caribbean include (from top to bottom) Nassau groupers, golden schoolmasters, gray angelfish and octopus.

plenty of fish to be encountered. They have mostly evolved as entirely different species to those found in the Indo-Pacific region. Caribbean species include the striped Nassau grouper and the large schools of yellow-striped grunts that loiter around reef tops. Other brightly colored fish that can be seen in groups include the golden schoolmasters. There are many types of angelfish that usually browse the coral heads in pairs. They include the yellow-and-black French angelfish and the gray angelfish.

Large, colorful tube sponges adorn the reef walls, where the water plunges to hundreds of feet deep. Some of the best dives of the Caribbean area are wall dives.

The ubiquitous common octopus stalks the reef top, looking for shellfish that form the majority of its prey. It always provides good entertainment as it can change its color, form and texture at a moment's notice to camouflage itself against the background of the seafloor.

If you are interested in the tiny and bizarre creatures that are often found in the seabed, the island of St. Vincent is rapidly developing a reputation as the macrolife capital of the Caribbean.

Grand Cayman is famous for its large population of southern stingrays.

Facilities

The islands of the Caribbean always provide good facilities for diving, and they usually have excellent flight connections with major hubs, such as Miami. They have some of the best and, consequently, most expensive hotels in the world, although it is also possible to visit on a small budget.

THE RED SEA

An amazing **variety of coral** grows on the reefs in the Red Sea, creating vibrant, multicolored formations for divers to explore.

Where is it?

The Red Sea is a flooded continuation of the Great Rift Valley between Africa and Arabia and is bordered on all sides by arid desert. The countries of Djibouti and Yemen form a narrow gateway to the Indian Ocean at its southern end, and Saudi Arabia makes up most of its eastern coastline. On the western side, Eritrea, Sudan, and Egypt form its borders. At its northern end, it splits into two gulfs. The Gulf of Aqaba leads to Israel and Jordan. The other is the Gulf of Suez, which connects to the Suez Canal.

Popular diving

The Red Sea is extremely deep and provides startlingly good visibility because detritus sinks away to the bottom. There are times, however, mainly around April, when plankton blooms temporarily disrupt the clarity of the water. Due to its proximity to Europe and the sympathetic political nature of its government, Egypt has proved exceptionally popular with divers. The Egyptian part of the Red Sea has probably the largest and most visible leisure diving industry anywhere in the world.

People can dive from the shore, take short trips on day boats or go on extended journeys to the more remote reefs on live-aboard vessels. The fleet of live-aboard vessels for diving is the biggest in the world and boasts more than 100 boats.

Red Sea life

Despite the vast numbers of divers that visit the Red Sea each year, the diving is still good. Hammerhead sharks, whale sharks, dolphins, manta rays and turtles are regularly spotted. The oceanic whitetip shark, once the most prolific large predator on Earth, is making a comeback and is often seen

A **green sea turtle** from the Red Sea. These long-lived creatures are an endangered species.

patroling the Red Sea reefs, just beneath the surface.

The reefs of the Red Sea are not only famous for their quantity of coral, but also for the varieties of different coral that grow alongside each other in such profusion. Among these, colorful soft corals are revealed

The vast variety of **animals of the Red Sea** includes, clockwise from top left, the far-ranging oceanic whitetip shark, soft coral, schools of anthias around hard coral and striped bannerfish.

THE SHARKS OF SHA'AB RUMI

Jacques Cousteau made the reef of Sha'ab Rumi in Sudan famous when he filmed his Conshelf 2 underwater-living experiment there. You can still see the remains of some of the buildings rusting away underwater where he left them. Sha'ab Rumi is a large circular reef with a lagoon that can now be entered by vessels thanks to Cousteau's adventures with explosives. Because it is surrounded by deep water, Sha'ab Rumi is a good place to encounter sharks that make their way on colder upwelling currents to the relatively shallow plateaus at either end of the reef. The few dive boats that visit this location are reputed to offer bait to the gray reef sharks in return for the sharks putting in an appearance.

---

in vibrant crimsons and delicate pinks as soon as a diver shines a light on them.

The fish life of the Red Sea is equally impressive, with several species that are indigenous to the area. Orange anthias flutter around the hard coral and yellow-and-black striped bannerfish gather in droves. Anemonefish bustle around their host anemones. In shallow areas where there is no coral, enormous green sea turtles graze on the sea grass. It's the lucky diver that gets an encounter with a grazing dugong, a relative of the manatee.

For all this, most of the Red Sea is not tropical. The northern border of the tropics passes close to the border with Sudan. The sea temperature can be quite chilly in winter months, requiring divers to wear thick suits. There is a strong northwest wind, and the surface of the water is rarely calm.

Egypt has good flight connections with international airports on its Red Sea coast at Sharm el Sheikh, Hurghada and Marsa Alam.

THE INDIAN OCEAN

The lagoons of the **Maldivian atolls** are ringed by a necklace of low-lying, palm-fringed islands.

The Indian Ocean is a vast tropical body of water that stretches from the coast of East Africa to the coast of Western Australia and is bordered by India and Indonesia in the north. It includes within it the islands of the Seychelles and Mauritius, the Laccadive Islands, Sri Lanka and the Maldives. All locations offer spectacular diving, but none is more popular than the Maldives.

The Maldives

The islands of the Maldives are coralline, growing on the rims of sunken, prehistoric volcanoes, or atolls. "Atoll" is a Divehi (the language spoken on the islands) word that has been adopted into the English language to describe the way the islands are ranged around a lagoon of calmer water. In Divehi, "atoll" actually means "administrative district." Each island is only a few inches above sea level, covered in coconut palms and surrounded by turquoise sea.

Giant **Napoleon wrasse** are curious about divers and like to take a close look.

Until the recent development of sophisticated tourism and hotel island resorts that rival the best of the Caribbean, the only industries of the Maldives were tuna fishing and scuba diving. Consequently, every holiday island is well equipped with an up-to-date diving center, and there is now a large choice of cabin cruiser dive boats, too.

All the atolls have world-class diving to offer, but Ari Atoll, South Male Atoll and North Male Atoll have the best. Strong currents force their way through the gaps between the islands according to the season

comeback after many years of depletion by
Chinese fishing fleets.

Ecological disaster

In 1998, the extensive coral reefs of the
Maldives were almost destroyed by coral
bleaching that is thought to have been
caused by a sudden rise in water
temperature. It has taken eight years for
some of the reefs to recover, but with or
without the coral, the channels between

Vast schools of blue-lined yellow snapper are
the signature fish of the Indian Ocean reefs.

and this brings both clear water and plenty
of nutrients to feed the marine animals.

Maldives marine life

Huge schools of blue-lined snapper mark
every reef in the Maldives. The giant
Napoleon wrasses are almost tame because
they encounter divers so often. Exotically
striped oriental sweetlips are just one species
of several types of sweetlips to be seen.
Manta rays glide between the reefs, feeding
on the plankton. These gentle giants come
into favorite reefs to allow smaller fishes to
clean parasites from their skin and gills,
which the cleaners do in return for a free
meal. The manta rays are very well organized
creatures, forming an orderly lineup to wait
for attention. Up to 40 animals have been
seen waiting their turn.

The feeding of sharks by divers to
encourage their appearance has now been
banned in the Maldives. However, shark
fishing has also been banned to some extent,
and the shark population is making a

the reefs still offer superb, world-class diving
thanks to the oceanic animals that are
attracted to the currents.

The best time to go to the Maldives for
diving is during the dry season, which is from
December to June. The currents are at their
strongest in January.

Spectacular yet gentle, plankton-eating manta rays
glide between the reefs and line up for attention from
small fish at known points along the reef.

THE PACIFIC REGION

The vibrantly colored soft coral of **Fiji's reefs** flourish in fast-flowing currents.

The Pacific Ocean covers a third of the surface of the Earth. It stretches from Asia and Australia in the west to the Americas in the east and from Russia and Alaska in the north to the Antarctic in the south. The Pacific region includes about 25,000 islands and is as varied and exciting as any diver could wish for.

Where to dive
Papua New Guinea is a haven for divers interested in weird and wonderful marine creatures. The Coral Sea off Australia includes the Great Barrier Reef, the world's largest coral reef system. The islands of Melanesia, such as Fiji, are renowned for their brightly pigmented soft coral.

The islands of French Polynesia are scattered over about 950,000 square miles (2.5 million square km), but their total landmass is only about 1,550 square miles (4,000 square km). The lagoons of French Polynesia are subject to the rise and fall of the ocean tides. The water rushes in and out of the atolls, attracting large numbers of sharks and other fish that feed in the currents. There are also giant clams and clownfish darting around the anemones.

A **cuttlefish** puts on a brilliant display of ever-changing colors (left). Every diver is thrilled to find a **seahorse** (above right). Schooling **batfish** swim above a reef (opposite).

A giant clam (left). Clownfish huddle, safe from the stings of their host anemone (right). A fast-swimming jack hunts tiny fish that hide in the coral (below right).

The Hawaiian Islands have large populations of manta rays.

Micronesia includes Palau, the Caroline Islands and the Marshall Islands. Bikini Atoll in the Marshall Islands has many famous wrecks that sunk after World War II in the first peacetime detonations of atomic bombs. Vanuatu has the famous wreck of the SS *President Coolidge*, a World War II troopship sunk at Espiritu Santo. The islands of New Caledonia have good diving, too. World War II has left an underwater legacy of wrecked ships and airplanes that have become undersea habitats for many animals. The lagoons of Chuuk (Truk), Palau, the Solomon Islands and the Philippines are punctuated with these human-made reefs that are fast becoming incorporated into the natural undersea topography. They all make great dive sites.

Near the equator, where the coasts of South America and North America meet, there are converging warm and cool sea currents. These help keep the climate of the islands of the Galápagos unusually equable. Because of the cool current coming from the south, the ocean here is cooler than you would expect. The sea around the Galápagos islands has as many varied and unusual examples of marine life as the islands have land animals. Divers can experience the thrill of swimming with equatorial penguins and marine iguanas.

Slightly farther north, the islands of Malpelo and Cocos enjoy cold upwellings that attract sharks normally only found in deep water to shallow depths. There, the sharks school, and divers can marvel at them. The islands are famous for vast numbers of hammerhead sharks, as well as huge populations of whitetip reef sharks and marble rays.

THE RICHEST REEFS

Raja Emphat, an archipelago of islands north of West Papua in the south-eastern Pacific, is a favorite location of photographers Larry and Denise Tackett. There, Dr. Gerald Allen, the well-known ichthyologist, made a record count of 283 fish species on the Cape Kri reef, the home reef of the Kri Island Resort. Dr. Jen Veron, a respected hard coral specialist, counted 400 out of 465 known species of coral on a single dive in the islands. In 2001, the Nature Conservancy, the World Wildlife Fund and Conservation International decided that Raja Emphat is the site of the world's richest coral reefs, yet Raja Emphat is still a relatively undiscovered part of the world.

DIVING WITH BIG ANIMALS

It's thrilling to swim alongside an ocean-roving leviathan such as the gentle, plankton-eating **whale shark**.

It's a thrill to find yourself diving alongside a creature that is bigger than you and totally wild, even if at first it seems daunting.

Diving with sharks

Of all the animals that experienced divers want to get close to, sharks are the first choice. However, an average shark encounter usually ends with the animal disappearing hastily into the blue. There are hundreds of different species of shark and certain places in the world where sharks can be reliably seen. These shark sites include the Maldives, the southern Red Sea, Polynesia, Micronesia, the Bahamas, and the islands of the Western Pacific. The most common shark species in warm coastal waters is the scalloped hammerhead shark, which often congregates in large numbers.

Other large animals

Sharks aren't the only large animals that divers can swim with. The seals of the Farne Islands in the United Kingdom and the sealions of Baja California in Mexico and the

Galápagos can entertain a diver with their acrobatic ballet for a whole dive.

At Grand Cayman in the Caribbean, southern stingrays know where fishing boats returning from trips out to sea stop to clean their catch, tossing unwanted scraps over the side. The rays congregate there to feed, and many dive centers soon discovered the location, too. Now, divers and snorkelers can enjoy close encounters with these intelligent animals that have learned to associate

A cruising **bull shark** should be treated with caution.

170

Scalloped **hammerhead sharks** can be found anywhere in the tropics where there are upwellings of colder water.

people with free food. They call the place Stingray City, and it has turned into quite a feature of the Cayman tourist industry. There are other places where this has happened, although they are less well known, including Gibb's Cay in the Turks and Caicos Islands and Manjack Cay in the Bahamas.

Turtles are always a favorite with divers, and hawksbill turtles can appear almost anywhere on a reef. Green turtles have a long lifespan and grow to a massive size. There is nowhere better to see turtles than the oceanic island of Sipadan, off the coast of Malaysia. Green turtles are also often seen grazing on the sea grass along Egypt's coast. Turtles breathe air so divers should never hold onto a turtle and stop it getting to the surface for a breath.

Cayman Island stingrays (above) are often curious about humans, whereas **green turtles** (right) browse the sea grass, seemingly oblivious to divers.

WHALE SHARKS

Whale sharks (*Rhincodon typus*) are the biggest species of fish in the sea. They are so-called because they feed by filtering the water for plankton and small fish in the same manner as baleen whales. Although they can grow to a massive 60 feet (18 m) in length, they are very docile animals. Those divers lucky enough to enjoy an encounter with a whale shark are invariably impressed both by its size and its approachability.

Whale sharks are often affectionately known as "spotty monsters." They have broad, flat heads, distinctive light spots and horizontal and vertical lines on their gray bodies. They roam the oceans of the world in pursuit of their food source, nearly always swimming near the surface. The Indian Ocean has a large population of whale sharks that migrate in a circulatory pattern from the Gulf of Tadjoura in the Horn of Africa, past the Seychelles and the coast of Mozambique, past Western Australia and through the Maldives back to the Gulf of Tadjoura, where they give birth. A separate population wanders the Pacific Ocean. The Galápagos, Cocos and Malpelo islands are good destinations to choose if you wish to dive with these creatures, although a whale shark can turn up almost anywhere in tropical seas.

SMALL IS BEAUTIFUL

A pair of colorful **nudibranchs**, or sea slugs, about to mate.

The Far East, mainly formed by Indonesia, Malaysia and Papua New Guinea, is famous for its vast catalog of marine life, with more species identified there than in any other area of the world. The creatures found in this region range from the tiny pigmy seahorse to the giant manta ray. North Sulawesi, Raja Emphat, Sipadan, Layang Layang and Loloata are all names famous, or soon to be famous, with traveling divers.

Muck diving

Lately, scuba divers have come to appreciate the tiny and obscure, even bizarre, animals that live in environments other than coral reefs. This type of scuba diving is called muck diving, and there is one particular place where it originated.

The strait between Lembeh and the mainland of North Sulawesi is not an idyllic stretch of water, twinkling limpidly and invitingly. It is a busy waterway frequented by thousands of small local boats, as well as assorted freighters and tugboats hauling barges, serving the nearby port.

But Lembeh Strait is special. There is nowhere quite like it; the site is littered with

A snake eel with its attendant cleaner shrimp (left). One of a hundred different varieties of frogfish (above right).

detritus dropped carelessly from boats for the past thousand years.

This is the place to find nature's outtakes. As you focus in on the grit and muck that makes up the bottom, you realize that it is actually heaving with life. A million different animals await you, and most are like nothing you have seen before. If it looks like a bit of trash, it's probably an animal camouflaged to look like its surroundings, or maybe it really is a bit of trash but with an animal living in it.

None of the creatures is very large, so you will need to get down and examine what lies in the rubble. It may help to use a powerful magnifying glass. You will need to look carefully—even a discarded plastic bag may provide a home for something. The rule is to dive with your eyes, not your hands. Many of these small animals are very venomous, but they are easy to photograph if you are circumspect about your buoyancy control. Almost everything seems to live on or in the sea bottom.

A **blue ribbon eel** seemingly gapes in alarm from its hole.

This tiny, rare, green fish is a **halemida ghost pipefish**, closely related to the seahorse.

What to look for

Lembeh Strait is not unique—most of the strange marine animals that inhabit its seabed can be found elsewhere. However, the sheer profusion of varieties of bizarre creatures is unusual, all found in such close proximity to one another.

There, you will see frogfish of all types— giant, hairy, warty and lots more. The many other unusual creatures include zebra lionfish, scorpionfish, flying gurnards, pufferfish and a lot of different nudibranchs,

scattered like brightly colored candy. Vibrant ribbon eels gape in alarm from the safety of their holes. Like so many Russian dolls, every animal seems to have at least one other creature living within it. At night, in pitch darkness, the rare little mandarinfish leaves the protection of the rubble to make a brief mating dance in mid-water, before dashing back to safety.

Muck diving is now popular at many other dive sites, partly because of the easy-to-use, compact digital cameras that record these tiny subjects so well. The island of St. Vincent claims to be the "critter" capital of the Caribbean.

The tiny **mandarin fish** only dashes out in the open when it is totally dark.

FAMOUS WRECKS

A World War II **Jake seaplane** sunk at its mooring in Palau (above).

In 1992, divers rediscovered the wreck of the SS *Thistlegorm*, where it lay in the Red Sea. This freighter had been sunk by enemy action in 1941 and was loaded with war supplies intended for the buildup to Operation Crusader—the British Army's drive to force Axis troops out of North Africa. Its cargo included trucks loaded with motorcycles, trains, airplane parts, rifles, ammunition, artillery shells and much else. The ship had lain undisturbed for 40 years; it had been dived and documented by Jacques Cousteau

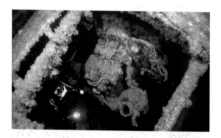

Inside the wheelhouse of Yamamoto's flagship, the *Nagato*, inverted on the bottom at Bikini Atoll.

BIKINI ATOLL

Bikini Atoll is the site in the Marshall Islands where atomic and hydrogen bombs were tested over 12 years from 1946. For the first atomic tests, the Americans gathered together an almighty fleet of 84 warships, redundant after the capitulation of Japan. One of the greatest fleets ever assembled, it was certainly the only one gathered with total destruction in mind. The vessels included the premier carrier vessel USS *Saratoga*, the captured German battle cruiser *Prinz Eugen* and Admiral Yamamoto's flagship, the mighty Japanese battleship *Nagato*. There were also submarines, destroyers, a World War I Dreadnought battleship, attack-transports, patrol boats and landing craft. They mostly now lie at the bottom of Bikini Atoll's lagoon, and it has become every wreck diver's dream destination.

One of the many British war-time motorbikes carried in the hold of the SS *Thistlegorm*.

in the early 1950s, but had then been forgotten. Lying upright at around 100 feet (30 m) deep, it is now probably the most visited wreck site in the whole world.

World War II saw many fleets of Japanese supply ships sunk where they had assembled. The most famous of all these locations is Chuuk, otherwise known as Truk Lagoon, but it is by no means the only location where American planes sunk Japanese ships. The lagoons of Palau are littered with sunken ships, including the "helmet wreck," a wreck that was discovered fairly recently and has become very popular.

Throughout all of the Western Pacific there are similar wreck sites. These include Hansa Bay in Papua New Guinea and Iron Bottom Sound in the Solomon Islands. Not only are there wrecked ships, but many of the airplanes that attacked them ended up in a watery grave as well. Everything from multi-engine bombers to fighter aircraft and even seaplanes lie on the seabed waiting for divers to visit. In Vanuatu, the wreck of the SS *President Coolidge*, an ocean liner turned troopship, lies underwater having sunk after hitting a mine.

Not all wrecks were the result of war. The *Bianca C* was an Italian cruise liner that caught fire in port while visiting Grenada. It was towed out to sea by a British warship before being sunk close to the beach, making it convenient for divers to visit. In Cyprus, a roll-on-roll-off ferry loaded with trucks got into difficulties and sunk just outside Larnaca harbor. The wreck of the *Zenobia* is regularly

visited by divers and is probably the most popular dive site in Cypriot waters.

The Red Sea is full of the remains of vessels that came to grief on reefs through errors of navigation. One reef, Sha'ab Abu Nuhas, at the gateway to the Gulf of Suez, is littered with the remains of vessels. These range from the wreck of the SS *Carnatic*, a P&O steam-sailing ship that dates back to 1869, to the MV *Giannis D*, a Greek-owned freighter that sank after hitting the reef in the 1980s. The SS *Yongala* is Australia's most famous wreck. It was a 357-foot (109-m) long steamer that tragically sank in a cyclone in 1911. The wreck lies inside the Great Barrier Reef, around 55 miles (90 km) southeast of Townsville.

Technical divers make expeditions to dive the remains of the British warships the HMS *Repulse* and the HMS *Prince of Wales* in the South China Sea. They also dive the wreck of the HMHS *Britannic*, the sister ship of the RMS *Titanic*, where it lies at the bottom of the Mediterranean Sea.

The plane elevator on the wreck of the aircraft carrier USS *Saratoga*.

175

ARTIFICIAL REEFS

Sinking unwanted vessels as artificial reefs has been an ecological success. It has proved cost effective because it reduces scrapping costs, and provided a vessel is previously prepared so that there is no risk of pollution, it represents a new and much needed habitat for marine life.

Where to find them
There have been hundreds of vessels sunk off the east coast of Florida as artificial reefs, and these have proved effective in reducing the effects of coastal erosion. A couple of natural reefs run the length of the state's eastern seaboard, but more notable is the long line of wrecks, about 2 miles (3 km) from shore. Yachts, aircraft, tugs, freighters and sections of oil rigs make up what is probably the most extensive artificial reef system in the world. They are all suitable for scuba diving.

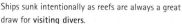
Ships sunk intentionally as reefs are always a great draw for visiting divers.

The boost to the local economy given by artificial wrecks has lead to other wrecks being purposefully sunk throughout the world. In the United Kingdom, there is the wreck of the HMS *Scylla*, a former Royal Navy frigate intentionally sunk for divers off Whitsand Bay near Plymouth.

Two decommissioned passenger ferries, 115 feet (35 m) and 184 feet (56 m) long, have been sunk within 160 feet (50 m) of each other in a position and depth that is suitable for the majority of scuba divers to visit which diving around the island Gozo, near Malta. Off the coast of Malta itself, a large disused oil tanker has been scuttled. An ex-Russian destroyer

All recently sunk vessels look similar, whether they were sunk by accident or design.

has been sunk in the shallows near to Cayman Brac in the Caribbean, and in Israel, a small, obsolete gunboat was purposefully sunk as a dive site close to the shore near the Coral Beach in Eilat. Aqaba in Jordan has its own artificial reef, the wreck of the MV *Cedar Pride*.

The Canadian Artificial Reef Society has overseen the sinking of six unwanted warships off the coast of Vancouver Island and even a Boeing 737 airliner to create underwater habitats. Cuban authorities have sunk a frigate in its coastal waters for the benefit of the diving industry.

The Bahamas has a huge selection of smaller vessels that were either abandoned by moviemakers after being sunk for specific movie projects, such as the Bond movies, or simply sunk for use as dive sites.

Diving an artificial reef

The main difference between diving an artificial reef and a "real" wreck is that because the vessels have been sunk purposefully, they have been cleaned of any polluting materials first. This ensures that no damage is done to the environment. The vessels are cleared of any hazards that might trap animals or divers, and often access holes are cut to allow safer penetration.

Of course, since artificial reefs are a relatively recent initiative, none of the wrecks have been submerged for very long, and there is little marine growth on the vessels yet. This may give the feeling that these are not proper wrecks, but this is how all wrecked vessels looked when they were first lost, whether by an act of war or poor decision making.

THE WORLD'S LARGEST ARTIFICIAL REEF

Sunk in 2006 near Pensacola, Florida, the "Mighty O" is the USS *Oriskany*—a decommissioned aircraft carrier of Korean and Vietnam War vintage that proved too expensive to restore as a floating museum of naval air warfare. It was sunk as the world's largest artificial reef instead.

The ship is about 900 feet (275 m) long and lies upright on a seabed that is 200 feet (65 m) deep. Its sheer size makes an all-around tour quite a daunting prospect for divers.

The *Oriskany* was a modern carrier vessel. It carried no big guns, nor was its control tower armored. Its aircraft were its armaments, and their range meant that the vessel could be kept as a floating airfield, well out of harm's way, with other escort ships doing picket duty to protect it. Initially deployed in the

Mediterranean in 1951, the *Oriskany* was later the first vessel of its type to pass around Cape Horn. It was continually updated and was one of the first carriers to have an electric escalator to carry flight crews to the upper decks quickly and easily. In 1961, it became the first aircraft carrier to be fitted with the revolutionary Naval Tactical Data System (NTDS).

Most divers are content to swim around its island superstructure. The flight deck, at 138 feet (42 m) deep, is as big as an airfield.

SHARK-INFESTED WATERS

Whitetip reef sharks are lethargic during the day but become highly voracious predators during the hours of darkness.

Years ago, scuba divers were taught that if they saw a shark they should leave the water immediately. Today, we are more enlightened. Experienced and inexperienced divers alike travel the world and are prepared to pay a premium to be guaranteed a close encounter with these often misunderstood predators.

Where to find sharks

Nowhere is this more evident than in the Bahamas, where shark diving has become an important part of the nation's tourist economy. This, in turn, has given the sharks

there a protected status. To date, one dive center alone has seen more than 60,000 divers enjoy close encounters with sharks without injury.

To make sure that the sharks turn up on cue, the animals are tempted in with bait in the form of scraps of fish. The main species of shark that attends these regular feeds is the Caribbean reef shark, and these sharks arrive in quite large numbers.

Caribbean reef sharks are the sharks often seen in movies, and many pictures featuring sharks have been photographed in the waters around the Bahamas. A Caribbean reef shark looks exactly as you would expect a shark to look. Most of the dive centers in the Bahamas stage shark-feeding dives, and

Caribbean reef sharks at a staged shark-feeding dive in the Bahamas (left). A scalloped hammerhead shark at Cocos Island (opposite).

these give divers the opportunity to see these spectacular animals closeup.

Divers are invited to sit in a circle around the feeder, who passes out the fish bait piece-by-piece on the end of a short spear. The sharks circle around in an orderly fashion, waiting their turn for a bite. The feeder usually wears chain mail gloves to avoid accidents.

Some parts of the northern Bahamas have healthy populations of bull sharks and tiger sharks, but if you want to see larger examples of these two fearsome species closeup, go to a shark-feeding dive at Beqa Lagoon in Fiji. There, the feeder simply pours

A hungry **Fijian bull shark** is a fearsome-looking creature.

The giant **tiger shark** is often thought of as the tropical equivalent of the great white shark.

COCOS ISLAND
Cocos Island, an uninhabited rocky outpost of the Eastern Pacific, is famous for its large population of schooling scalloped hammerheads. Divers who patiently wait by cleaning stations are often rewarded with closeups of these strange-looking sharks. These big animals come in to locations where smaller fish act as "manicurists," picking off parasites from the sharks' skin. The water around Cocos Island also has a vast population of whitetip reef sharks. They loll around lazily during the daylight hours, but once darkness has fallen, they become voracious predators. The sharks have learned to use the lights of visiting divers; the light mesmerizes smaller fish to the advantage of the sharks in their nighttime hunt for a meal.

fish blood into the water before handing out big pieces of dead fish. The Fijian dives may attract up to eight different species of shark. You may see bull sharks—these fierce-looking creatures are the stuff of nightmares. Even more nightmarish are the adult tiger sharks, some of which may be 20 feet (6 m) long.

There are organized shark-feeding dives that attract gray reef sharks and silvertip sharks in French Polynesia and elsewhere around the globe. In fact, anywhere that has organized shark-feeding dives attracts sharks that are usually less timid of divers than normal. You may even be lucky enough to see sharks swimming close to you even though there is no food on offer at the time.

HEALTH HAZARDS

It may surprise you to know that a far greater number of people on vacation in the tropics are killed or seriously injured by falling coconuts than are ever hurt while diving! There are a number of hazards to be aware of when planning for or taking part in a dive trip.

Malaria
The tropics may look idyllic, but the region harbors a number of endemic diseases. The most dangerous animal by far is not the shark but the mosquito. In some places, such as the Solomon Islands, 30 percent of the population suffers with malaria, which is spread by the bite of the carrier mosquito. Malaria is a serious and life-threatening disease. To avoid being bitten, you should

It may be romantic and look idyllic, but dusk is when malaria mosquitoes do the most damage.

If you choose to sit below a tropical palm tree, watch out for falling coconuts!

cover your skin in the evenings and at night with light clothing and use an insect repellent that contains DEET.

You should sleep under mosquito nets if they are provided, but most importantly, you should plan ahead. It is essential to use the correct anti-malarials for the type of malaria endemic to the region. The anti-malarial medications proguanil and chloroquine are rarely effective now as in many places the malaria parasite has developed resistance to them. Some doctors recommend mefloquine, but it can have unpleasant side effects, including hallucinations, that make it unsuitable for use by scuba divers. Malarone or doxycycline-based treatments are good alternatives. The World Health Organization provides guidelines for doctors about which drugs to prescribe, depending upon the area being visited. The drugs must be taken in advance of the vacation.

Sun damage
Sunshine is another serious problem that can lead to disastrous consequences. You should not expose your body to too much sun and should avoid overheating, especially when shore diving. You should put your suit on just before entering the water and find shade as soon as you leave it. Sunstroke can occur

Sunstroke occurs when the body overheats, so get to the shade as soon as you can.

when the body's mechanism to rid itself of excess heat is overwhelmed by a very hot or humid environment, or even strenuous physical activity.

People particularly susceptible to sunstroke are young children, the elderly, individuals not used to physical activity and excessive sun exposure, people suffering from certain chronic medical conditions and those involved in sporting activities. The symptoms include an increased body temperature with hot, dry skin, hyperventilation, mental confusion and possible unconsciousness.

Other hazards

Even in cooler climates, precautions should be taken. For example, there are many diseases that are endemic to freshwater sites, and you should be careful not to swallow any water. Wherever you are, if you cut yourself, you should take care. Seawater is loaded with bacteria, and it can easily get into your body through a break in the skin's epidermis, the outer barrier against infection. You should cover even the smallest abrasion with a watertight adhesive dressing. Cuts made by coral can be particularly invasive. Injuries not dealt with quickly can end up being serious.

Waterborne diseases are common at freshwater sites so try to avoid swallowing any water.

A FIRST AID KIT FOR THE TROPICS

There are various companies offering ready-made first aid kits for travelers. One of these, the eMed kit, can only be used in conjunction with a doctor's consultation that may be given by e-mail.

The kit contains a variety of medical equipment, such as sterile syringes and needles, dressings, a scalpel, antiseptic powder and cream, lignocaine, hydrocortisone cream, various broad-spectrum antibiotics, pain relief, treatment for diarrhea, antihistamines, anti-vomiting drugs and anti-inflammatory pills.

In addition, rehydrant powders, decongestants, aftersun soothing lotion, vinegar for stings and waterproof adhesive dressings should be carried. In some remote areas, your own supply of blood plasma substitute may be advisable. It is also vital not to forget to take out reliable diving and medical insurance.

USEFUL ADDRESSES

TRAINING AGENCIES

International Association of Nitrox and
Technical Divers (IANTD)
1545 NE 104 Street
Miami Shores, FL
33138-2665
www.iantd.com

National Association of Underwater
Instructors (NAUI)
PO Box 89789
Tampa, FL
33689-0413
www.nauiww.org

Professional Scuba Association (PSA)
www.scuba-training.net

Scuba Schools International (SSI)
2619 Canton Court
Fort Collins, CO
80525-4498
www.ssiusa.com

Technical Diving International (TDI)
Scuba Diving International (SDI)
18 Elm Street
Topsham, ME
04086
www.tdisdi.com

Professional Association of Diving
Instructors (PADI)
PADI International Ltd.
Unit 7, St. Philips Central Albert Road
St. Philips, Bristol
BS2 OPD
United Kingdom
www.padi.com

PADI Foundation
9150 Wilshire Boulevard, Suite 300
Beverley Hills, CA
90212-3414
www.padifoundation.org

British Sub-Aqua Club (BSAC)
Telford's Quay, South Pier Road
Ellesmere Port, Cheshire
CH65 4FL
United Kingdom
www.bsac.com

Verband Deutscher Tauchlehrer (VDTL)
Hartwig Sachse
Maria Mann
Gudensberger Straße 3
D-34295 Edermünde
Germany
www.vdtl.de

MEDICAL AGENCIES

Divers Alert Network (DAN)
The Peter B. Bennett Center
6 West Colony Place
Durham, NC
27705
www.diversalertnetwork.org

Undersea & Hyperbaric Medical Society
(UHMS)
10020 Southern Maryland Boulevard
Suite 204
Dunkirk, MD
20754
www.uhms.org

Divers Alert Network (Europe) (DAN)
PO Box DAN 64026
Roseto (Te)
Italy
www.daneurope.org

Diving Diseases Research Centre (DDRC)
The Hyperbaric Medical Centre
Tamar Science Park, Research Way
Plymouth
PL6 8BU
United Kingdom
www.ddrc.org

USEFUL ADDRESSES

South Pacific Underwater Medical Society
(SPUMS)
c/o Australian and New Zealand College of
Anaesthetists
630 St Kilda Road
Melbourne
VIC 3004
Australia
www.spums.org.au

DIVING MAGAZINES

Rodale's Scuba Diving Magazine
www.scubadiving.com

Sport Diver Magazine
www.sportdiver.com

Undercurrent
PO Box 3120
Sausalito, CA
94966
www.undercurrent.org

Asian Diver
MediaCorp Publishing Pte Ltd.
Techpoint #01-06/08
10 Ang Mo Kio St 65
Singapore 569059
www.asiandiver.com

Dive Pacific
PO Box 42-020
Orakei, Auckland
New Zealand
www.divenewzealand.com

Diver Magazine (UK)
55 High Street
Teddington
TW11 8HA
United Kingdom
www.divernet.com

Diver Magazine (Canada)
www.divermag.com

DYK
Diver Group Scd. ApS
Thoravej 13
3 DK-2400
Copenhagen NV
www.dyk.net

H2O Magazine
Red Sea Association for Diving & Watersport
Tourist Center Villa 18
Hurghada
Red Sea
Egypt
www.h2o-mag.com

Octopus
www.octopus.ru

Scuba Diver Australasia
Asian Geographic Magazines Pte Ltd.
20 Kramat Lane
04-04 United House
Singapore 228773
www.scubadiveraustralasia.com

OTHER

The Historical Diving Society USA
PO Box 2837
Santa Maria, CA
93457
www.hds.org

The Historical Diving Society
Little Gatton Lodge
25 Gatton Road
Reigate
RH2 0HD
United Kingdom
www.hds.com

GLOSSARY OF TERMS

A

A-clamp: The international method for attaching a regulator valve to a tank valve.

air bank: A method of storing large quantities of compressed gas.

algae bloom: Plant plankton that causes the water to be turbid.

algorithm: Mathematical calculation used in a diving computer.

alternate air source: An air source other than your primary regulator.

Archimedes' principle: The effect of the displacement of fluid relative to an object sinking or floating.

artificial ventilation: A method of keeping air flowing through a non-breathing casualty's lungs.

ascent rate: The approved speed at which a diver comes up through the water column.

atmosphere: The pressure caused by the weight of the atmosphere at sea level.

B

bar: An accurate metric measure of pressure to which one atmosphere at sea level approximates.

Beaufort Scale: Used to express wind speed.

bezel ring: A rotating grooved rim of a watch used to calculate time intervals.

BC: Buoyancy compensator.

blue hole: A flooded cave system; also called a cenote in South America.

Body Mass Index: An expression of weight against height.

Boyle's Law: Relates to the changing volume of gases under changing pressure.

breathing rate: Mean respiratory volume.

buddy: A partner who accompanies another diver underwater.

buddy check: When one diver checks his or her partner's equipment.

buoyancy: Whether a body sinks (negative) or floats (positive).

buoyancy check: A method by which a diver can check to adjust ballast weights.

C

camband: A band that is stretched by way of a cambuckle to hold a tank to a BC.

carbon dioxide: The poisonous waste gas of oxygen metabolism.

cardiac compressions: A method used to maintain circulation of blood in a casualty without a natural heartbeat.

closed-circuit: Equipment that does not cause gas to be exhaled out into the water.

compressor: A machine used to fill cylinders with breathing gas.

current: Water that is moving in a definite direction.

current hook: Allows a diver to stay stationary and hands-free in a current.

cylinder test date: The date at which a cylinder was last tested.

D

Dalton's Law: Relates to the pressure of individual gases in a mixture of gases such as air.

decompression illness: Caused by absorbed nitrogen forming gas within the tissues before it is returned to the lungs for exhalation.

decompression stop: A pause during an ascent to allow absorbed inert gas to return to the lungs.

deep stop: A decompression stop that is made deeper than traditional methods normally suggest.

demand-valve: The regulator valve that gives you gas in volume and pressure exactly as you demand it.

direct-feed: A hose that supplies air to an accessory directly from the diver's tank.

diving computer: An instrument that automatically calculates decompression status.

DPV: Diver propulsion vehicle.

drysuit: A diving suit that is designed to keep a diver dry.

DSMB: A delayed-deployment surface marker buoy.

dump-valve: A valve for releasing air from a BC, drysuit or lifting bag.

E

ear clearing: The act of making a Valsalva maneuver to equalize pressure in the middle ear to that of the outer ear.

emergency swimming ascent: An ascent where the diver keeps his or her airway open so that expanding air can escape freely.

F

fin kick: The method of using fins for propulsion.

free diving: Diving by simply holding a breath.

free-flow: When a regulator sticks open allowing air to freely escape.

G

gas absorption: The ability of a liquid to absorb gas under pressure.

gas analyzer: An instrument for determining the content of a gas mix.

H

H-valve: Two tank valves attached to a single tank that allow two entirely separate regulators to be used.

helium: A rare, lightweight inert gas that is substituted for nitrogen when deep diving.

Henry's Law: Relates to the absorption of gas while under pressure.

HID: High intensity discharge light, which produces a great amount of illumination.

hood: Worn to keep the head from losing heat to the water.

GLOSSARY OF TERMS

hyperventilation: Breathing faster and deeper than normal.

I

integrated-weight system: A weight-system built into a BC.

J

jetboots: A propulsion system that is attached directly to the diver.

L

latex seal: A thin rubber seal that is used in conjunction with a drysuit to stop water passing through.

lifting bag: Inflatable bag used to lift objects off the seabed.

live-aboard: A vessel that is self-sufficient so that it need not return to port every night.

lung expansion injury: Caused by holding a breath while ascending through pressure reducing changes.

M

MOD: Maximum operating depth for a particular breathing gas.

multilevel: Ascending during a dive so that it is conducted at progressively shallower depths.

N

neap tide: A tide that has a smaller difference between high and low water levels.

nitrogen: An inert gas and the greater part of the air we normally breathe.

nitrox: A mix of oxygen and nitrogen with increased levels of oxygen.

no-stop time: The maximum time allowed at a particular depth whereby a diver may make an ascent, without stopping, to the surface.

O

O-ring: A small rubber ring with an O-section, used as a water or air seal in a joint.

octopus rig: An alternate air source.

open-circuit: Equipment that allows expired air to bubble freely away into the water.

oxygen: The gas that is used in metabolism.

oxygen toxicity: Oxygen can be poisonous depending on its pressure and the length of time you are exposed to it.

P

partial pressure: The pressure exerted by a single gas within a mix of gases such as air.

pony: A name for a small redundant cylinder of breathing gas used in case of emergency.

R

rebreather: Equipment that is designed for the diver to rebreathe the same gas.

regulator: The valve that regulates your air supply to match the pressure of the surrounding water.

reserve pressure: The remaining pressure of gas in a tank.

S

seasickness: The confusion of senses leading to nausea and vomiting.

semi-dry suit: A wetsuit that tends to keep the water out through the use of seals.

shotline: A line held by a weight and supported by a buoy at the surface.

SMB: Surface marker buoy.

spring tide: A tide with the greatest difference between high and low water, with strong tidal movement as the level changes.

square-profile: Diving down to a single fixed depth before returning to the surface after an interval of time.

strobe: A flashing electronic light used as a visual emergency signal.

submarine housing: A watertight case that contains an item in an air-space maintained at atmospheric pressure.

surface interval: Time spent at the surface between dives.

swim line: The line on a compass that indicates the direction to swim.

swim platform: An area at the aft of a vessel that is low and designed to allow easy access to the water.

T

tank: Another term for a cylinder or transportable pressure vessel.

technical diver: A diver who uses special techniques to extend the range of diving beyond normal leisure diving depths.

tissue half-time: The time it takes for a theoretical tissue model to become half-saturated with gas at that pressure.

toxins: Poisons used as defence mechanisms by some animals to disable an attacker.

trilaminate: Two layers of material bonded either side to a waterproof butyl layer.

trimix: A breathing gas made up of oxygen, nitrogen and helium.

twin cylinders: Two cylinders bonded together and used as one or independently as two.

U

underwater search: A systematic method for finding a lost object.

W

weightbelt: A belt with a quick-release buckle onto which ballast weights can be attached.

winder reel: A bobbin and ratchet onto which long lengths of line can be wound or unwound.

wing: A BC that keeps all its flotation characteristics at the back.

INDEX

Main entries are indicated by **bold** numerals